The Journey
from
Brokenness
to
Belovedness

OUR THREE SELVES

Andrew Lawson, MD

Dedication

This book is dedicated to:

The God who continually, wholeheartedly, unconditionally pursues us and whispers to each of us, "You are my beloved."

My bride who continues to pursue me and whispers to me, "You are my hero."

My kids may you never forget that God has tattooed on your hearts before you were born, "Beloved".

To all of you who have joined me on this journey from brokenness to belovedness.

Our Three Selves

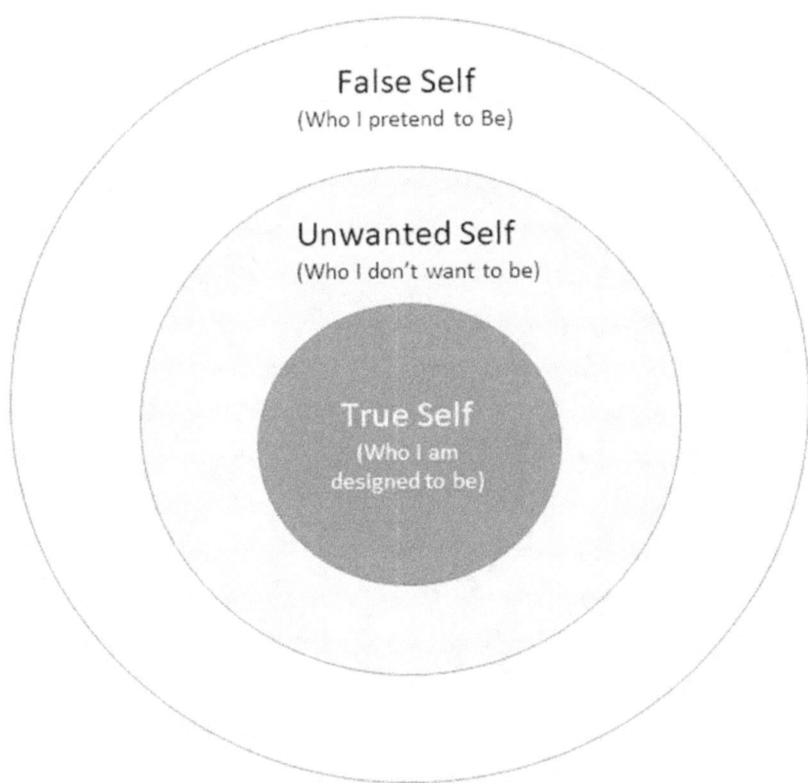

false self — Who I pretend to be.
unwanted self — Who I don't want to be.
True Self — Who I am designed to be.

Table of Contents

Rules of Engagement

I want to share some agreements or "rules of engagement" that I want you to establish with yourself as we proceed.

Rule One: Apply NCRW.

The first rule is NCRW, which stands for Naturally Creative, Resourceful, and Whole. It is one of the pillars of coaching from my coach training with the Co-Active Training Institute.

My training as a medical doctor focused on finding deficits—finding out what is wrong with the patient and how to fix the problem. In that process, you quickly see others as people who are broken and need to be fixed. I don't think physicians are alone in this view of the world.

It was a breath of fresh air to question this assumption. During my first day of coach training, this concept was introduced. We are *not* beings who are fundamentally broken and in need of fixing, but rather we are beings who are naturally creative, resourceful, and whole. We don't need to be fixed.

What a wonderful lens to see the world through. Approaching ourselves and those around us with this view can be transformative. When we try to fix everything, we miss the true potential of any relationship.

NCRW in Action, Example One:

During my coach training, one of the trainees was being coached by a master coach. The trainee began to cry, and all of us were there to observe. Half of us immediately reached for the box of tissues for the trainee.

The master coach stopped us and said, "The trainee is NCRW. So if she feels that she needs a tissue, she will get one herself."

NCRW in Action, Example Two:

I have coached executives who check their email every few minutes. I encourage them to only check their email twice per day, advice that is often taken with hems and haws. The few who give it a try find that, given time, many problems are solved by those sending the emails. The senders are fully capable of figuring out solutions on their own.

NCRW is seeing yourself and others as beloved, created in the image of God, not broken and needing fixing. How you see others will determine how you lead and listen to them and to yourself.

Rule Two: Throw Out "Looking Good and Getting It Right."

The second rule comes from a coach training course that I took in 2014. Before the people in our group began working together, the master coach held her palms up and said, "Throw out looking good and getting it right." She acted as if she was throwing something over her shoulder, first with her left hand, then with her right hand.

In 2019 during Daring Way Certification Training, Brené Brown pointed out that we are held back by our fear of scarcity, comparison, and shame. "Getting it right" is a fear that if we don't get it right—according to whatever we judge as" right" in our minds—we will be laughed at or judged according to someone else's answer. There are no right or wrong answers as you work through this content.

Rule Three: Have a Beginner's Mind.

Beginner's Mind is a meditation term from the East— simply meaning to approach this content with a mind of a child, a beginner, someone without any preconceived notions or judgments.

Rule Four: Be Fun, Easy, and Buoyant.

Remember to approach this with fun and ease instead of with serious, solemn, heavy-lifting countenances. In other words, be buoyant. In one of my coach trainings, the instructor started by asking, "How do you want to be with one another?" One of the participants said, "Buoyant. We want to lift up one another. If one of us is struggling, we will step in to lift them up."

Rule Five: If you're comfortable, you're not learning.

To get the most out of this content, we might need to lean into some discomfort. You may remember taking classes in school that made you uncomfortable, because the content was complicated. Our brains like routine, but for us to learn anything new, we must nudge them into places where they have never been before. This makes our brain work harder than it would like, and it makes us feel uncomfortable.

Rule Six: Practice Self-Empathy.

As best as you can, practice self-empathy. Set aside the inner critic who whispers in your head that you are broken, you are not good enough, or you're a failure.

We must all learn to let go of that inner critic and instead listen to the voices that whisper in our heads that we will be okay just the way we are. We are NCRW. We don't need any fixing right now.

Do we talk to ourselves like we talk to our kids, to our spouse, or to our closest friend? We must change our self-talk to a voice of kindness and empathy.

"Self-empathy enhances resilience, transforming our relationship with ourselves from harshness and judgment to kindness and self-compassion. It includes handling stress and emotional pain, finding peace with unmet needs, and healing our inner critic." — Oren Jay Sofer

We will be talking about ourselves and things that "tweak" us. These things largely stem from events in our lives that—for whatever reason—made us feel isolated, disconnected. These events are described by Brené Brown as shaming events.

"If you put shame in a petri dish, it needs three ingredients to grow exponentially: secrecy, silence, and judgment. If you put the same amount of shame in the petri dish and douse it with empathy, it can't survive." — Brené Brown

As we begin this journey together, we must remember that the antidotes to our shame, to our unwanted and false selves, are transparency (opposite of secrecy), vulnerable sharing (opposite of silence), and non judgment, non attachment (opposite of judgment).

For us to feel safe, as we explore ourselves together, empathy is the *key* ingredient.

Andrew Lawson, MD

Kristin Neff, a self-compassion researcher and professor, believes there are three components to self-empathy.

1. Self-kindness is the language where we talk to ourselves like we are talking to someone we love. We all have unwanted and false self "voices" talking to us all the time. We must learn to manage these voices in our heads so when they speak, we can begin to hear them as soft, silly, and mostly silent.

2. Common humanity recognizes that we're all experiencing similar things. We all have similar neural networks and pathways, so we're not alone in any of this.

3. Mindfulness tells us to slow down and recognize what our brains are doing so we can actually rewire our thoughts.

A homie, Shaggy, once texted me: "The curious paradox is that when I accept myself just as I am, then I can change." — Greg Boyle[1]

Rule Seven: Make Connections.

1. A key part of this journey is *connection*, not only to ourselves but to others.

2. We must remind ourselves that we are *not* alone in our struggles, in our woundedness.

We need to realize that our unwanted and false selves are *not* unique to us. We *all* struggle with similar unwanted and false selves. The only way to know ourselves and others is by being connected to others. We need to find safe people and share this journey with them, because we all have sat on "that bench."

One day he came to work and plunked himself down in my office. "Last night, I was walkin' home from King Taco," he said. "You know, on Soto. Anyways, before I get to my canton, I'm crossing in front of that tiny park. You know the one. I see an old man lying on a bench. He's either asleep or tryin' to sleep. There's a half-full forty on the ground in front of him and the old guy, well, he's shiverin' cuz it's cold. So you know my favorite sweater?" I nod yes, though I don't know what he's talking about. I don't want to derail him. "Well, I was wearin' it, and I took it off and laid it over this guy. He didn't wake or notice." For a moment, Andres enters a sort of trance. And then suddenly he's shaken from it. "Hey, I'm not tellin' ya all this so you think I'm AAALLLLL that." He stops again to think, and some long-held emotional stirring comes to the surface, making it momentarily hard to get the next words out." Nah, I'm tellin' ya all this cuz I know that bench." — Greg Boyle[2]

Rule Eight: Practice Journaling.

We should never overlook the value of journaling. I use the Day One app (www.DayOneApp.com) for journaling, but many of my clients use Evernote (www.Evernote.com) or OneNote (www.OneNote.com).

Studies have shown that journaling is an excellent way to enhance our brain's ability to clarify and set down ideas.

Simply asking people to write about their most upsetting negative experiences for fifteen to twenty minutes to create a narrative about what happened, if you will, leads them to feel better, visit the doctor less, and have healthier immune function. By focusing on our experiences from the perspective of a narrator who has to create a story, journaling creates distance from our experience. We feel less tied to it. — psychologist James Pennebaker[3]

Introduction

I want to give a brief sketch of the three circles diagram and what each of the circles represent.

The innermost circle is our True Self circle. We each have a True Self that is unique to us. There is only one Drew Lawson True Self on the planet. We will discover and fill in this innermost circle with all the unique attributes of *you*. As I say to my clients, "We want you to make decisions, influence others, and live your life from your Drew-ness (insert your name here: _________-ness)."

The next circle is our unwanted selves' circle. If our True Self is filled with all that makes us beloved and unique, our unwanted selves' circle is filled with our broken pieces. For me, this is filled with "I am *not* enough! I would *die* if anyone saw me as stupid. I do *not* want to be seen as needy." We will also explore and fill in this circle with a list of each of our unwanted selves.

The outermost circle is our false selves' circle. If our unwanted selves are those parts of us that we don't want anyone to know about, our false selves are their opposite, which we display to the world to try and cover up our unwanted selves. One of my unwanted selves is *stupid*. I hate to look *stupid*. Therefore, I have a false self who looks and acts really smart. We will clarify each of our false selves as we move through the content.

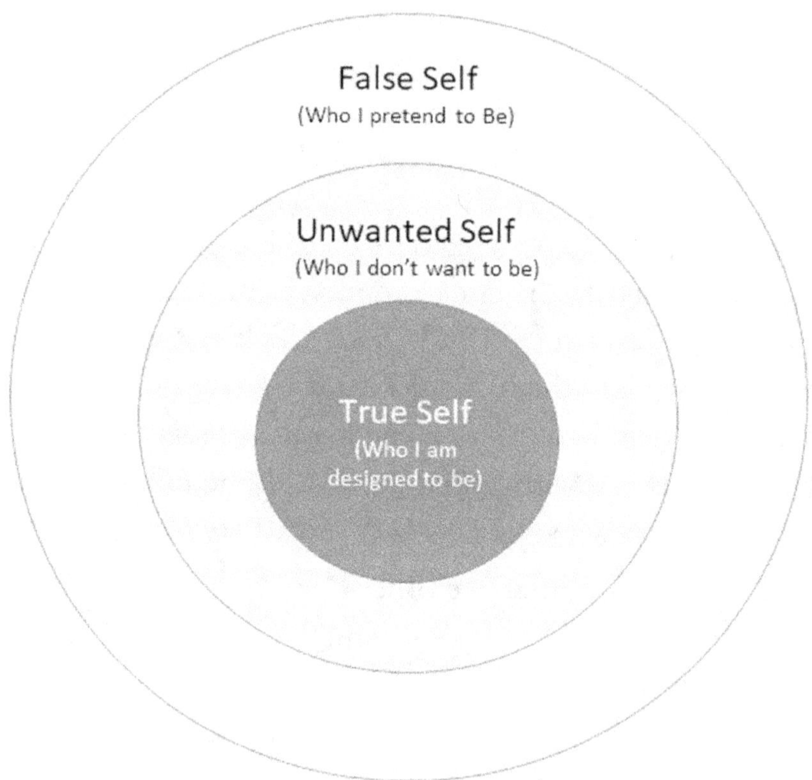

false self — Who I pretend to be
unwanted self — Who I don t want to be
True Self — Who I am designed to be

Letting the self emerge is the essential task of leaders.
— Warren Bennis, contemporary thought leader[4]

In the core of our being, we are a singular True Self comprised of a unique set of attributes. However, over time our True Self atrophies (shrinks) as we develop a set of personalities (masks) or what I refer to as *unwanted and false selves*. We will be looking at our True Self and our other selves who are created by our synapses, experiences, and stories.

Executive Coaching and Leadership Development from the inside out.

I am proud to work with the Building Champions coaching company with its unique value propositions. We have learned that leaders are only as good as the decisions they make and the influence they have. Their influence and decisions come from the inside, not outside—from the leader's thought patterns. This is why the CEO and founder of Building Champions, Daniel Harkavy, always says, "Self Leadership precedes Team Leadership."

Before we can begin to lead others, we must first develop ourselves as leaders. The content that we will be diving into will help each of us become better leaders and better humans.

Most people never pay much attention to the ultimate source of a happy life, which is inside, not outside.
— Dalai Lama[5]
We don't see things as they are, we see them as we are.
— Anais Nin
In reality, the self is the only place to begin. If we are not at home within ourselves, we cannot make grounded,

conscious choices. When we are unfamiliar with the diverse terrain of our own internal landscape, our options will be fairly limited. — Co-Active Leadership by Karen and Henry Kimsey-House

Self-Awareness

Self-awareness is the foundation for great leaders. Our willingness to develop our self-awareness determines our ability to develop as leaders. This is the starting point for all leadership development. We can't develop our teams without first developing ourselves, and with that comes the ability to self-correct.

If we can't self-observe, then we can't self-correct.
— Christopher Heuertz
Self-awareness is the most important leadership capability.
— MIT's Sloan Management School

I have learned that if you take a bunch of executives and ask them how self-aware they are, they will give themselves high marks. Some studies have shown that they'll place themselves in the ninetieth percentile on self-awareness. However, the people around them will often tell you that they are actually in the tenth percentile in self-awareness.

This is true for all of us. I think it's important for us to embrace and recognize that as we go through this, one of the most important tools for a leader is to be self-aware and to develop that muscle.

Self-awareness has two components: internal self-awareness & external self-awareness. Our internal self-awareness is our ability to recognize, clarify, and embrace ourselves: True Self, unwanted selves, and false selves, and the beliefs and behaviors driven by them. Our external self-awareness is our ability to recognize how other people experience us. How do you actually come across to others (not how you think that you do)? The good news is that both the internal and external can be learned and developed. As we focus on the internal, the external will be strengthened.

All of coaching is about awareness. Here is an acronym I learned: 'A.T.E.B.A.R.'

A-Awareness of

T-thoughts

E-Emotions

B-Beliefs, leads to

A-Action, leads to

R-Results

My purpose statement for my coaching practice is "to walk along side my clients as they recognize, clarify, and embrace their brokenness and their belovedness." Self-awareness is knowing our belovedness and brokenness and leaning into both. It is learning HOW to think not what to think.

We lead more out of who we are than out of what we do. . . . If we fail to recognize that who we are on the inside informs every aspect of our leadership, we will do more damage to ourselves and to those we lead." — Peter Scazzero[7]

If we don't get in touch with who we are, our design, our neurochemistry, and our thought and belief patterns, then we will do harm.

Sadly, many of the things that undermine our joy and happiness we create ourselves. Often it comes from the negative tendencies of the mind. . . . We create most of our suffering. — Dalai Lama[8]

A very important book, *Positive Intelligence* by Shirzad Chamine, points out that we cannot expect change if we don't address our thought patterns.

Billions of dollars are wasted on training and development each year. Within six months of most expensive trainings . . . many participants can barely recount what they learned or point to what has changed. Most of these trainings focus on higher-level competencies, while leaving the deeper underlying (negative thought patterns) intact. For example, in conflict-management workshops, people learn active-listening skills and work hard at listening to one another better. The problem is that if the nasty (thought patterns) are left intact, it will soon override any benefit derived from active listening. Your new active-listening skills might even become a tool used by (our negative thought patterns) to gather better evidence against the other person. As one leader put it to me, "If you enter this workshop a jerk, you will leave a jerk, except you are more dangerous now because you will know better how to cover it up. — *Shirzad Chamine* [9]

Unfortunately, most Leadership Development is focused on what many call the "Outer Game", our behaviors, but when we focus on the outer game, no change occurs. It is only when we can rewire our inner game of thinking, feeling, and believing that we can transform the leader to make the best decisions and optimize their influence.

We must strive to know the inner workings of our brain chemistry and learn to unwire and rewire our neurons because otherwise NO training will help, and in fact, it might hurt us.

Every several months at the hospital and healthcare system that I have worked at for over two decades, there is a new behavioral training. Much of coaching involves individual and team training sessions. But all of this content is worthless and harmful unless we get our inner neurochemistry right.

If you can imagine yourself as an iceberg. Most coaching focuses on the tip of the iceberg that is above the water surface. This tip is what the world sees of us, our behaviors. The vast majority of the iceberg is under the surface. Our thoughts, beliefs, and feelings are all under the surface, and we cannot become better leaders of ourselves or others without focusing on these.

Andrew Lawson, MD

Hearing Voices

In a scene from the Disney Pixar movie *Inside Out*, a family has moved to San Francisco from a midwestern city, and the daughter is struggling to adapt. The movie personifies five primary emotions that talk to each of the characters throughout the movie.

In this scene, the thriving emotion of joy is missing, so the survival emotions of fear, sadness, anger, and disgust have stepped in to dominate her internal conversations. You see unwanted and false self voices popping up in the caricatures of these emotions. The young girl's True Self is represented by the character in her brain, known as Joy. Because Joy has gone missing, her unwanted and false selves have taken over her emotions, beliefs, and thinking.

It is a great movie to watch to help us better understand the complex voices going on in our brains. All those neural networks are talking to one another, like the voices in our heads.

Our brains are exceedingly complex, and the neural pathways that develop for our unwanted and false selves have become very strong, with incredible bandwidth, because they have gone unchecked for many years. These advanced pathways sound like somebody is talking to us inside our head—a little voice that makes up stories and statements that become deeply embedded in our brain.

16

Do you hear them? Our advanced brain, called the neocortex, takes neurochemical signals and converts them into the voices that we hear in our heads, such as: *You're Stupid. Don't do that. This is going to fail. You are not enough.*

Our unwanted selves' voice says, "You're stupid."

Our false selves' voice says, "Look and act smart. Pretend."

Our True Self voice says, "You are a curious, lifelong learner."

The Know Yourself Schematic

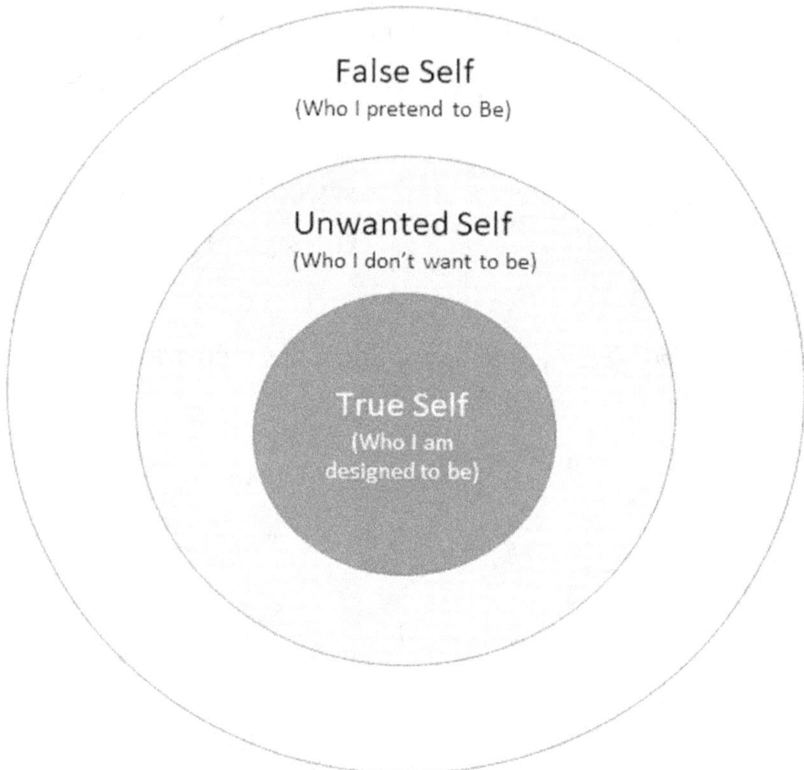

This is the schematic that we are going to use as a template for our work together. I hope that each of us will have this schematic front and center and begin the journey of filling in the white spaces on the schematic with our knowledge of our selves.

These are our three selves. Before we are born, we are designed to lead from our True Self, our essence, the unique set of attributes that make up who we truly are. However, as we grow and develop, we start to lose sight of our True Self because of events that occur in our lives. Unfortunately, and at times fortunately, we are storytelling beings. Our big brains take events and create stories from them. The stories that we tell ourselves lead to the formation of our unwanted selves which, in turn, cause us to create our false selves, and before we know it, we have shrunk our True Self circle and made our unwanted selves' and false selves' circles huge and impenetrable. Eventually, we not only don't know or recognize our True Self, but our True Self shrinks until it doesn't even show up anymore. All our interactions come from either our unwanted selves or our false selves.

True Self

The inner circle is who we were designed to be. It is our uniqueness. It is the part of us that combines to make the one and *only* person who we are. A unique, onetime, combination of DNA.

We will take the time necessary to rediscover our True Self. Sadly, most of us have no idea who we truly are.

Unwanted selves

This is the next circle moving outward. Brené Brown describes our unwanted selves or identity as that self that is trying to answer the statement: "I do *not* want to be perceived as . . ."[10] Huertz in his enneagram work[11] talks about each enneagram type having a specific fear. This fear goes into this circle.

False selves

The outer most circle is filled with our false selves. These selves are what we project to the world to help protect us from exposing our fear. They answer the statement: "I WANT to be perceived as . . ." These false selves are like the protective big brothers to our unwanted selves, an attempt to try and cover up, disconnect, hide, and protect our unwanted selves.

True Self is singular, because we have only one. However, unwanted selves and false selves are plural because we have many unwanted and false selves.

Current Reality Schematic

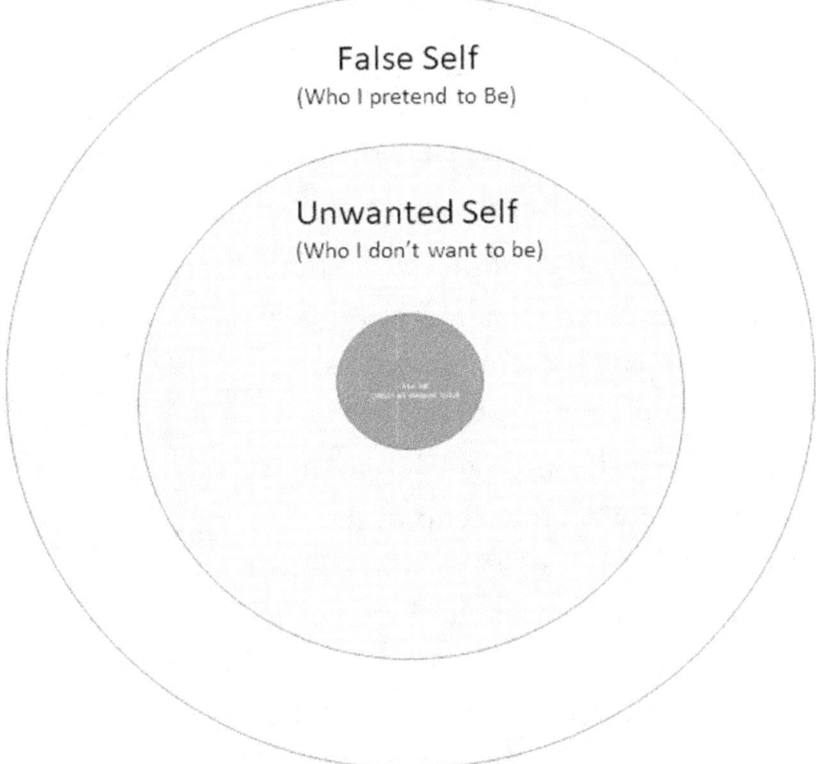

false self — Who I pretend to be.

Unwanted self — Who I don't want to be.

True Self — Who I am designed to be.

This diagram shows how most of us live our lives. We have a very, very small True Self circle, because we don't know who we truly are, and we have very large, robust unwanted selves' and false selves' circles. They go unchecked and unexamined, and for most of us, they are unknown. The outermost circle filled with our false selves are our masks or *persona*—a Greek word

for the large masks that early Greek actors used to portray their characters.

Our false selves' circle becomes so large and wide that we are essentially wearing hoop skirts or a huge sumo wrestler blow-up suit. These hoop skirts or sumo suits are so wide because all we're doing is bumping into one another's edges of our false selves. Our conversations and meetings are largely made of people not really being present but who are actually sending in their false selves. I often ask my clients, "Which one of your false selves showed up to the meeting?" Author of *Positive Intelligence*, Shirzad Chamine, has said that over 75 percent of us are not really showing up to meetings, but in our place, we send one of our false selves. He would argue that you have not truly met or interacted with *any* of your co-workers. Incredible.

The Goal

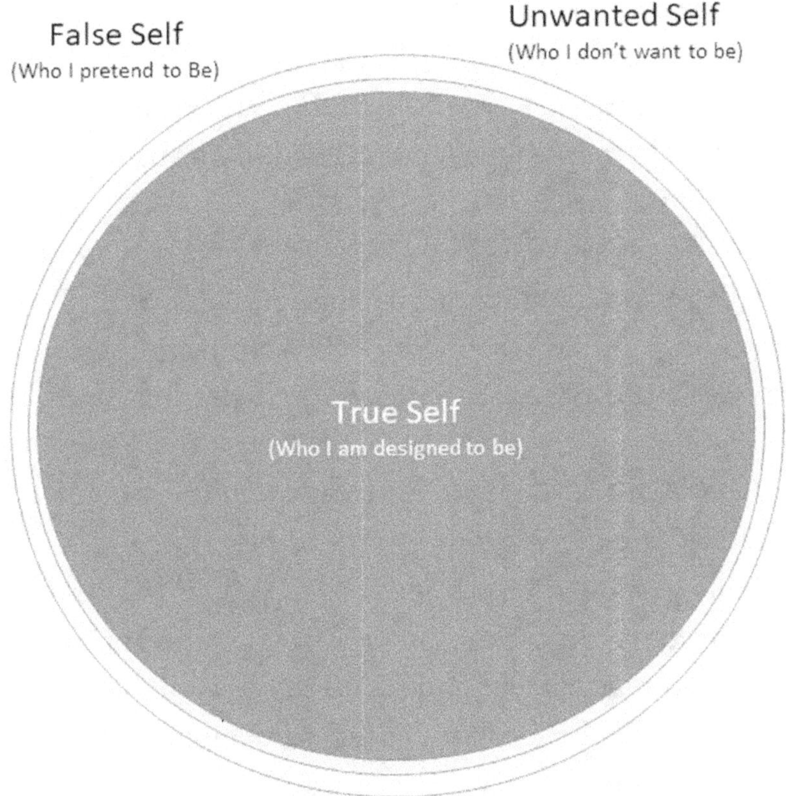

Our goal is to get rid of our false selves' circle—or at least make it very small and thin. While making our unwanted selves' circle as small as possible, we want our True Self circle to be as *huge* as possible. We will be exploring our circles, and we will journey toward this schematic.

We are born with our True Self circle being the largest of all the circles filled and infused with our belovedness, our unique combination of superpowers. Unfortunately our early childhood experiences lead to our brain making up stores which bring about unwanted and false selves.

My desired result for our time together is to get all of us to lead from our True Self while being aware of those stories and synapses we have created in our unwanted and false self circles.

As we explore and learn our different selves, we will be able to speak authentically from our True Self, expanding our True Self circle while shrinking our unwanted and false self circles to be paper thin so we can finally truly show up.

The ultimate goal is to have only two circles: our True Self circle being very large and highly developed and our unwanted selves' circle being paper thin and translucent to the world. Brené Brown and Daniel Coyle have been right all along in their emphasis on vulnerability. I believe the reason vulnerability is so important is because we must embrace, live, and wear our unwanted selves. They are our brokenness, and we must "wear" our brokenness on our "sleeves." We must be willing and vulnerable—able to share our unwanted selves to the world. Until we lean into our brokenness—that is, our unwanted selves—and are willing and able to be vulnerable with others, we will remain tethered to our false selves. We want our inner circle of True Self to shine like the unique diamond that it is with its one-of-a kind cut, color, and glimmer *and* with its unique flaws (unwanted selves) for all the world to see.

As we start our journey together, I wanted to share two examples of how this process can work, and a few examples of what the final product might look like.

This is an example of a final product from one of my former clients. It is my desire that we all leave our time together with such a completed project, so please start now with a diagram that you can continue to fill in along our journey together.

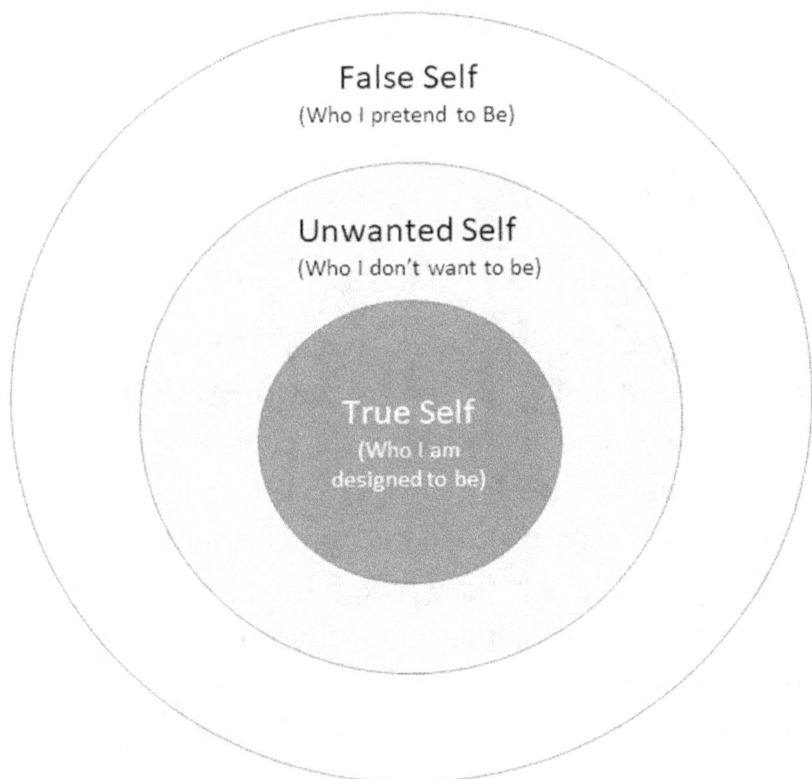

false self — Who I pretend to be.

1. people pleaser
2. scientist

3. organized
4. strong

unwanted self — Who I don't want to be.

1. pleaser/complier/not assertive
2. imperfect/flawed
3. rigid
4. anxious

True Self — Who I am designed to be.

1. confident
2. fierce
3. loved
4. vulnerable
5. beloved by God

As you can see, his center True Self circle is filled with beautiful, unique adjectives and phrases that reveal his True Self. The unwanted selves' circle has many different unwanted selves in it, with one that he chose to focus on—flawed and imperfect. His outer false selves' circle is largely filled with responses to all his unwanted selves. A common theme you will see with an unwanted self of   flawed" is its big brother as a dominant false self of   perfect"—being, looking, and acting perfect.

If he is not mindful, he will have the tendency to allow his perfectionism (a false self) to go to all his meetings and interactions with others. In fact, he made himself a bracelet that said "do it messy" to remind him to let go of his perfectionism. He has made the effort to literally wear his unwanted self, his brokenness, on his sleeve.

Another example of these selves comes from my own diagram. My True Self or my Drew-ness would have adjectives inside of my True Self circle of *curiosity*, *lifelong learner*, and others. A primary theme embedded in my unwanted selves' circle is *stupid*. This unwanted self does *not* want to be seen as stupid, no matter what. No surprise that one of my dominant themes in my false selves' circle is that of looking and acting smart.

How does this play out in my own life?

A doctor calls, and I'm about to tell them about an admission to the hospital. Their first response is, "Well, why didn't you give fluids?" I can immediately feel my body being triggered and one of my unwanted selves interpreting what this doctor has said as, "Hey, this doctor just called you stupid." This leads to that false self that I have named "Spock," who always looks and acts smart, to jump in and tell this doctor off and point out, in a condescending way, all the reasons why giving fluids would be the *wrong* and *stupid* thing to do. Now if I effectively manage my unwanted and false selves, I will respond to this doctor's question from my True Self and be curious and eager to learn why this doctor thinks giving fluids is the right way to go.

We are trying to get all of us to make our decisions from our, center, True Self circle. Later, we will unpack this more.

Discussion Questions

1. Draw your three circles in proportion to how they are currently.

2. Draw your three circles in proportion to how you want them to be.

3. Have a drawing of your three circles that you can use as a template to take notes and add to as we proceed.

4. Which circle do you think you currently live in the most? Why?

5. Which circle do you want to live in? Why?

6. How can you get yourself into that circle?

7. What questions do you have?

8. What are you really curious about?

9. How are these circles influencing your decisions?

10. Which circle(s) does your identity, self-worth, and safety live?

Please take the time to play with these questions. Don't worry if you can't answer all of them.

unwanted selves

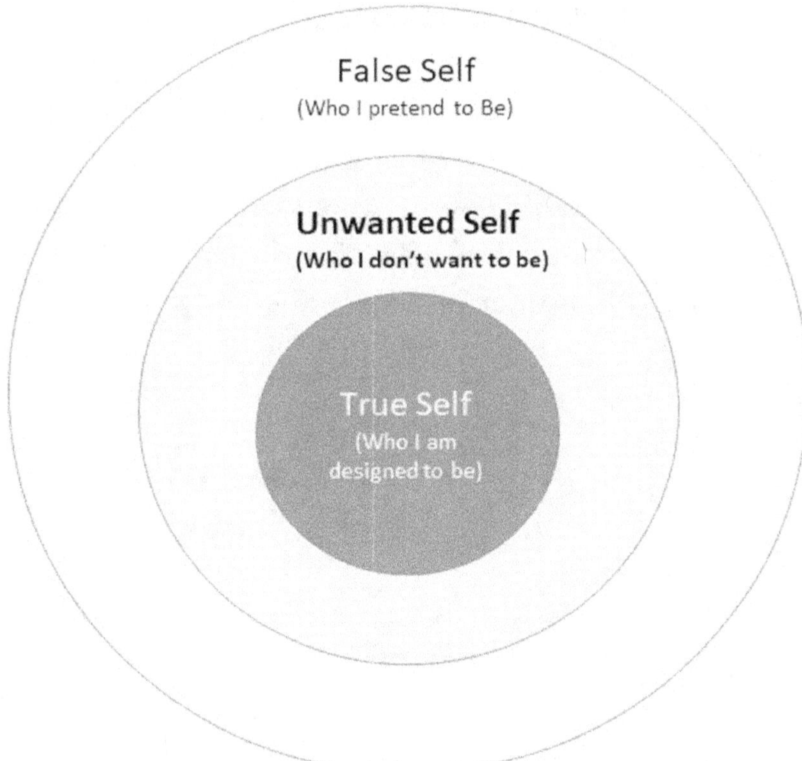

false self — Who I pretend to be.

unwanted self — Who I don't want to be.

1. Stupid, incompetent, incapable, needy
2. Not enough (The Jerk)

3. **Wrong (and everything must be right or wrong) (Bobby Binary)**
4. **Lazy**
5. **Overwhelmed (Splat man)**

True Self — Who I am designed to be.

This is a diagram of my different unwanted selves. I discovered them over years of working with myself, practicing, and going through coursework and coaching.

Unwanted selves form from a combination of our genetics and environment, and when influential people in our formative years tell us how we should be or what we should be doing. Once that is established, we create our false selves to hide our unwanted selves from the world and from our True Self. The psychologist Carl Jung spoke of this unwanted selves part of us as our shadow self.

Such a man knows that whatever is wrong in the world is in himself, and if he only learns to deal with his own shadow [unwanted selves], he has done something real for the world. — Carl Jung[12]

To confront a person with his shadow [unwanted selves] is to show him his own light. — Carl Jung[13]

"When we refuse to own our shadow, often it ends up owning us." — Christopher Heuertz[14]

Why Do we develop these unwanted selves?

Our unwanted selves develop during our developmental years. During early development, our brains process the world as a big and, at times, scary place. This causes our brains to lay down neuro networks (synapses) that translate experiences into fictitious stories and turn the volume up on our survival instincts. The combination of our over stimulated survival mode and the stories our brain makes up eventually leads to our brain trying to answer certain statements.

Survival Mode

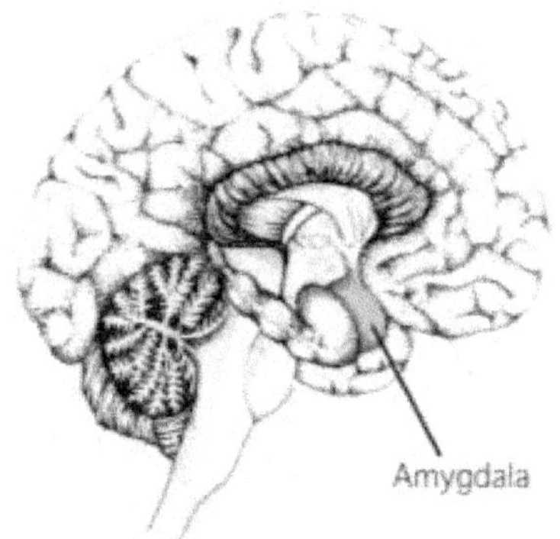

Before *anything* gets into our advanced part of our brains, it must first go through our amygdala, the feeling center of our brain. This is why brain scientists remind us that we are *not* thinking creatures that feel; we are feeling creatures who think.[15]

Or as Harvard psychologist Professor Horney says, "Go against, go away from, or go toward."

Andrew Lawson, MD

Our unwanted selves stem from our amygdala responses. The almond-shamed part of our primitive brain that scans our environment five times per second asking, "Am I safe? Is this familiar?" When our brain perceives our environment as unsafe or unfamiliar we respond in one of three ways: fight, flight, or fawn (also known as tend & befriend).

According to neuroscientists, everything from the outside world—all our senses—are funneling in from the outside world directly to our amygdala. Our amygdala is the gatekeeper to our brain, and this part of our brain was designed in this way so we can survive. If there's a trigger, your brain is designed to immediately respond to the threat so you stay alive.

Now if you are a bunny rabbit chewing on grass and you see a fox, your pea-sized brain says, "Unsafe, unsafe. Unsafe!" And this signal shoots down to the glands that excrete adrenaline and cortisol (stress hormone) so the bunny is ready for flight. The bunny certainly *never* chooses to go against a fox or go toward (befriend) it. It takes the go away or flight response.

Now if the fox leaves, then the bunny goes back to eating grass and has no further thoughts about a fox.

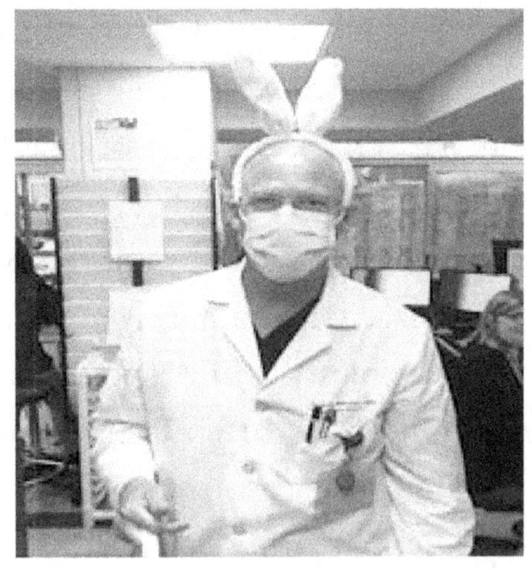

Unfortunately for us, we don't have it that simple. Our brain is larger than the pea-sized brain of the bunny, so our brains talk to us, asking questions such as, "Where did the fox go? Did it go to my house? Is it going to eat my kids? Am I loveable to the fox? Am I smart enough? Am I a success to the fox?"

Like the bunnies, we were designed to survive, and to survive, our brains are wired to *watch out* for harm.

The National Science Foundation says people have 12,000 to 60,000 thoughts per day. Over 80 percent are negative, and 95 percent are the same repetitive thoughts as the day before.

Our amygdala senses anything unsafe and unfamiliar, our bodies respond in flight (away from); freeze, tend, and befriend (go toward); or fight (go against). We gravitate toward one of these three as we develop our identity, because one of these three gave us the most safety. Unfortunately, we couple one of these three with our identity, safety, and self-worth, causing much of our adult angst and formation of our unwanted selves.

We each possess a "dominant" or primary unwanted self based on these three primitive responses to feeling unsafe. This survival mode is driven by fear. In most animals, it is simply fear of being eaten, but in our case with our advanced brain, the person with a fight response predominantly fears failure. The person with a predominant flight-response fears having and being enough which often translates to fear of being stupid or wrong. The person with a freeze response, which in advanced mammals is manifested by tending and befriending or fawning rather than freezing, translates this fear to feeling unlovable or unaccepted.

When our amygdala gets hijacked, it signals to our advanced brain, "Unsafe!" Our advanced brain then responds by asking one of three questions:

- Am I a failure?

- Am I stupid?

- Am I unlovable?

These are three of our unwanted selves. [16] [17]Each of us is feeling one of them more frequently than the rest.

How the stories in our heads create our unwanted selves:

When our amygdala signals "unsafe," it sends a message to our advanced brain, the neocortex, which morphs this message into what seems like a voice in our head, and that voice develops a story or fable. Our neocortex's story or fable response to our primitive mantra of fight, flight, or fawn develops in us and shapes us.

Don't believe everything you think. — Tim Ferris[18]

We crawl into these fables and let a sentence or a paragraph, which may have originated thirty or forty years ago and never been objectively tested and verified, represent the totality of our lives. — Susan David, PhD[19]

Our brain is a lazy, meaning-making machine, so instead of memorizing the exact event that triggered us to feel unsafe, our brain makes up a story. These are the origin stories of our unwanted selves.

For me, it was the spring of 1980 when I had a social studies project due. I had put in a lot of time into handwritten responses on a poster board, only for my dad to come home and tell me that there was a better way to do that. I tell this story of my dad tearing up my poster, but I am pretty sure he didn't actually do that. But it felt like he had. It was just an event in which my dad gave me great advice, but my brain made a story out of the event. In this story, my dad is saying, "You are not enough. You are not smart enough. You should have known better. You can do better."

This is fascinating, because some people might process this same experience with, "Hey, dad's telling me I am a failure (an unwanted self), and therefore I've got to look successful (a false self)." While others might create a different story in their brain chemistry with, "Hey, dad's calling me unlovable (an unwanted self) and I better be lovable (a false self)." And in my case, it was, "Hey, dad's calling me stupid and not enough (an unwanted self). So I better be enough and be smart (a false self)."

That was the embedded story my brain decided to create. This story is deeply engrained in my neurochemistry, and my dominant unwanted self comes from this story. There's the message: I'm stupid. I'm not enough. And then there's the story embedded with it.

My second embedded story that helped shape one of my unwanted selves was when I got lost in Palo Alto in the fall of 1985. I was a freshman water polo recruit at Stanford University. After my first practice, I got on a moped to go to a family in Palo Alto who was housing us during preseason training, only to get totally lost. The following day I was called "lost in" instead of Lawson. Again, just an event but one that was made into a huge story in my brain. This embedded unwanted self message said, "You are needy. You are incompetent." That message came from the event in 1985, which my brain created into a story or fable.

Scientists used to think our brains saw our environment like a photograph or a video, but our "view of the world is no photograph. It's a construction of [our] brain that is so fluid and so convincing that it appears to be accurate" (Lisa Feldman Barrett, PhD).[20]

My brain had developed or "constructed" the unwanted selves of neediness and incompetency. Forever after, my brain has embedded these unwanted selves as things to be avoided at all cost, things that signal "unsafe!" to my brain and body.

Our unwanted selves are formed from our genes, our environment, *and* our own special lens that we use to interpret the events in our childhood and beyond.

Shame can also contribute to the creation of our unwanted selves.

Brené Brown believes our unwanted selves develop from events that made us feel shame or shame triggers. We all can remember the events in our lives that triggered shame in us. Thankfully, we don't remember all these events, but the ones that we do imprint in us as unwanted selves.

I agree with Professor Brown when she says, "Sometimes we perceive others as assigning these unwanted identities to us, and other times, we pin them on ourselves. . . . Many of our unwanted identities that cause us to feel shame (and develop our false selves) stem from messages we heard growing up and from the stereotypes we were taught by our parents or immediate caregivers."[21] I can tell you that in my family "being stupid" was clearly an unwanted identity/self.

Finally, combining our brain stories and survival mechanisms our brain seeks to answer the following statements: "I would *die* if people thought I was (fill in the blank)." In Brené Brown's book *I Thought It Was Just Me*, she uses the following sentences to help identify what she calls our "unwanted identities":

- I am not ______________ enough.

- I do not want to be perceived as ____________.

- I don't want to be seen as ____________.

- I don't want people to think I'm ____________.

- I couldn't stand people thinking I'm ___________.

I have found my own answers: stupid, incompetent, needy, weak, foolish, lazy, and more. You will see that we are all together in this. Most of our unwanted selves are the same or similar. We *all* have a laundry list of unwanted selves.

UNLOVABLE

I would DIE if people saw me as . . .

A FAILURE

STUPID

We all carry around a large backpack of unwanted selves. An easy place to start is to recognize a "dominant" unwanted self that is constantly (without our knowing) saying to us one of three things: I would *die* if I was seen as either unlovable, stupid, or a failure.

As we develop, our huge neocortex starts to translate the three primitive responses into three fears or three core beliefs:

- I am not successful=I fear failure

- I am not lovable=I fear rejection

- I am not smart=I fear being inferior/stupid

I use the plural term unwanted selves because we each carry around more than one unwanted self. However, I believe we each have a dominant unwanted self that comes from our primitive survival brain message: fight, flight, or fawn.

Which one of these three unwanted selves dominates your thoughts?[22]

Remember, our brain is lazy. It likes to conserve its energy, its glucose. The way it does that is by making a lot of simple if-then statements. Remember:

- If they see me as really smart, then I'm okay.

- *If* I am lovable, *then* I am safe and secure.

- *If* I show them how successful I am, *then* I am worthy.

unwanted selves discovery #1:

1. How would you complete this statement: I would *die* if people thought I was . . .

2. What does this unwanted self mean to me?

3. Why is it so unwanted?

4. Where did the messages that fuel this identity come from?

5. What is the relationship between my unwanted selves and my identity, safety, and self-worth?

6. How does my unwanted selves influence my decisions?

7. What are your unwanted selves?

8. Write out the story that goes with each of your unwanted selves.

9. What would a Wanted Poster look like for each of your unwanted selves?

What triggers our unwanted selves

Triggers are those people, places, or circumstances that "set you off." They cause your unwanted selves to whisper in your head, "Hey, that person or circumstance is *unsafe* or bad, or that person is saying you are stupid, unlovable, or a failure." But in truth, they aren't.

My list of unwanted selves' messages is long. I do not want to be perceived as stupid, not enough, wrong, or needy. My dominant one is not wanting to be perceived as stupid, so a trigger for me is my unwanted selves' interpretation of someone's actions as directly or indirectly calling me stupid. The cardiologist who asks during a consult, "Hey, Drew why did you choose that blood pressure medication for this patient?" That's a harmless enough question—unless one of my unwanted selves interprets it as, "Hey, stupid Drew, why did you choose the wrong blood pressure medication for my patient?"

What do we do when we get triggered? Unfortunately, we usually choose disconnection, and there are many ways that we disconnect. Our disconnection strategies lead us to our outer circle of false selves. Our main form of disconnection is to listen to our unwanted selves' voices. One of my unwanted selves might say, "Hey, that cardiologist is calling you stupid—again." One of my false selves' voices will follow with, "You need to show him how smart you are by laying into him with a smart reply." We develop these unwanted (and false selves), and we allow them to run our lives.

The healthy and resilient action when we are triggered is to use a connection strategy. These connection strategies lead us into our inner circle of our True Self.

Knowing your unwanted selves triggers is a *key* way to rebound quickly and be able to choose between disconnection from others and True Self or connection to others and our True Self.

It is thought that the celebrated psychiatrist Viktor Frankl once said, "Between stimulus and response, there is a space. In that space is our power to choose our response. In our response lies our growth and our freedom."

Unwanted selves' discovery #2: Create unwanted selves' trigger grid

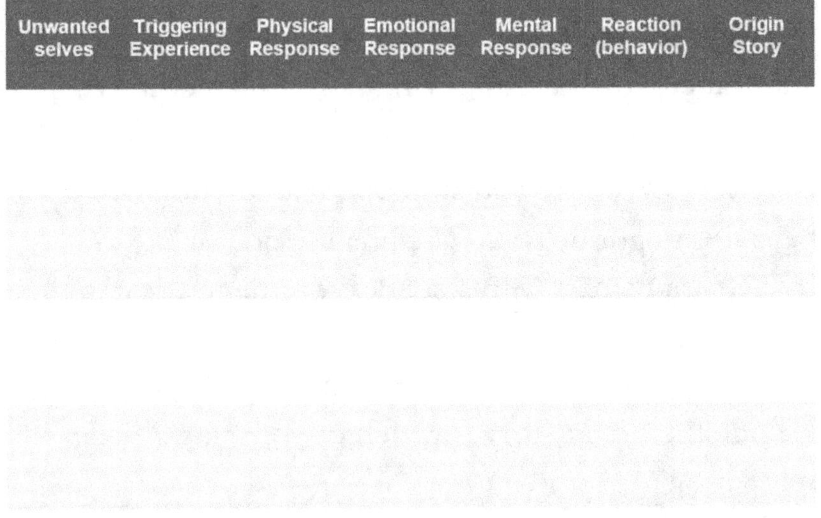

Unwanted selves	Triggering Experience	Physical Response	Emotional Response	Mental Response	Reaction (behavior)	Origin Story

This homework is to recognize our unwanted selves and the person, place, or circumstance that trigger our unwanted selves.

For example, here's a grid I would like you to start working with and working through. If I were to do this homework, a triggering experience would be a doctor at my hospital asking about giving intravenous fluids to one of my patients, and saying, "Why didn't you give fluids?" This can easily trigger my unwanted selves that interprets this comment as, "This doctor is calling you stupid." I'm sitting there on the phone, and this is the story funneling through my head: "Is she calling me stupid?" This is a triggering event. For the next few weeks, carry a grid like this on a 3x5 card. Jot down what happens in each of these categories when you feel triggered. What's your physical response when you feel an unwanted self shows up for you? For me it's flushes of heat. My emotional responses might be anger, annoyance, frustration, or irritation. The mental responses might be thoughts of telling her off with a comment like, "Are you stupid?" The reaction or behavior might be yelling, telling the doctor off, or trying to act smart with a snarky comment. Clearly, this behavior is not as successful as if we were functioning from our True Self. The last column is to remind you to include the origin story for each of your unwanted selves.

Here is a list of questions to ask yourself during this process:[23]

1. What is the Triggering Experience: Person, Place, Circumstance?

2. Physical Response: What does your body do when triggered? Where do you feel triggered in your body?

3. Emotional Response: What emotions come up when you are triggered?[24]

4. Mental Response: What story plays in your head? Where do you think that story originated? What phrase pops into your unwanted selves' circle when you get triggered?

5. Reactive Behavior: What do you do when you get triggered?

6. Origin Story: What is the origin story for each of your unwanted selves?

Below are some examples of physical, emotional, mental, and behavioral reactions when getting triggered, from Oren Jay Sofer's book *Say What You Mean.*[25]

Physical

- tightness in your jaw

- tension in your limbs or body

- shallow or rapid breathing

- flushes of heat, sweating, or cold

- feeling disembodied, ungrounded, or "up in your head"

Emotional

- fear, anxiety, annoyance, or a feeling of aggression

- irritation, anger, annoyance, or a feeling of aggression

- an urge to protect, explain, or defend yourself

- feeling frozen, overwhelmed, or stuck

Mental

- thoughts or images of anger, hate, or negativity

- thoughts for images of hopelessness or despair

- thoughts or images of worst-case scenarios

Verbal (reaction/behavior)

- an increase in the pace, pitch, or volume of speech

- reluctance to speak or respond, withdrawing verbally

- "but . . . that's not what I meant . . ."

- "You don't understand. You're not listening."

- "should . . . never . . . always . . . right . . . wrong . . ."

If you still are not sure why you feel triggered, remember that at least one of your unwanted selves will fall into one of three "buckets": (1) the stupid, not enough, bucket, (2) the failure bucket, or (3) the unlovable, imperfect bucket. Start to work through events in your life and those neural chemical pathway voices—those storylines that are being told to you internally, in your head.

These are a series of deeper questions to assist you:

1. What triggers your unwanted selves (person, circumstance, place)?

2. What happens in your mind, body, heart (feel), when your unwanted selves get triggered?

3. When your unwanted selves get triggered, do you usually go toward your True Self (connection) or your false selves (disconnection)?

4. What can you do to prevent your unwanted selves from getting triggered?

5. What can you do when your unwanted selves get triggered?

6. How well do you influence and make decisions when you are triggered?

This is a mnemonic that Pema Chodron shares in her book *Welcoming the Unwelcome*. It is a great way to help process through our unwanted selves' triggering events.

L.E.S.R.—"laser"—Locate, Embrace, Stop, Remain

1. Locate it. Investigate where that grasping, contracted sensation dwells in your body, and make contact with it.

2. Embrace. Embrace that feeling, that sensation, that contraction . . . send any fearful, grasping, self-protective feelings your unconditional warmth. This can be similar to calming a hysterical child. The main point is to reverse the ancient human tendency to avoid and reject pain. Instead you move toward it with heart.

3. STOP the storyline. Letting go of, interrupting, or looking directly at the thoughts and stories . . . go beneath or behind your thoughts to contact the underlying sense of being hooked . . . once you've connected with that raw feeling, you can then continue to interrupt the stories that keep you returning to the experience again and again.

4. REMAIN. Stay present with the feeling. Keep going until it shifts, or until it feels like too much of a struggle.[26]

unwanted selves' discovery #3: explore unwanted selves' origin stories

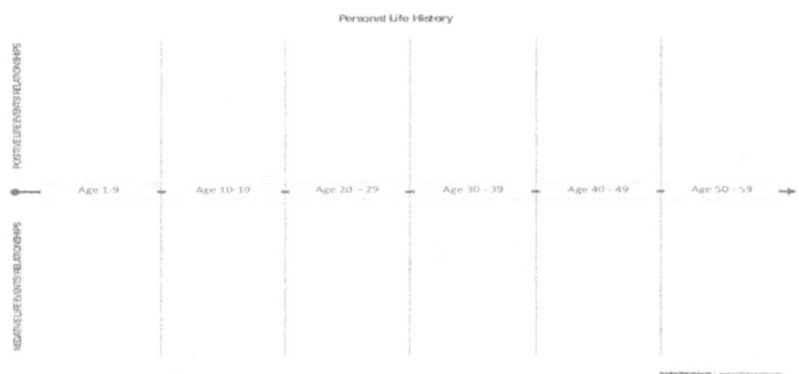

This homework is to look at your stories and the major highs and lows in your life through each of your decades. For example, between age ten and nineteen, I would have both the storylines that I have shared with you.

I would guess that most of our unwanted selves' storylines embedded in our brains are going to be from our first twenty to thirty years. Maybe not, but the key is to start to process and think about the storylines that developed your unwanted selves.

Using the timeline, what are those events in your early years that spawned one of your unwanted selves to emerge? How do they relate to your unwanted selves.[27]

false selves

false self — Who I pretend to be.

1. **Look Smart and Capable (Spock, The Tin Man, Answer Man)**

2. **I am enough (You are not enough) (Billy the Bully)**
3. **I am right/everything is wrong (The Judge)**
4. **Hard working/carry everything (Bag Boy/Backpack Man)**

unwanted self — Who I don't want to be.

1. Stupid, incompetent, incapable, needy
2. Not enough (The Jerk)
3. Wrong (and everything must be right or wrong) (Bobby Binary)
4. Lazy
5. Overwhelmed (splat man)

True Self — Who I am designed to be.

As you can see from my circles, many of my false selves are hyper-rational, intellectualizing everything. They have developed to protect the little kid in me, the unwanted selves in me who are worried and terrified of looking or acting stupid.

After our unwanted selves are established, our brain protects us from these unwanted selves and keeps others from seeing them by creating a group of false selves.

Our false selves usually layer on top of our unwanted selves. We will see a common theme unfolding that many of our unwanted selves will have a "big brother" false-self opposite.

Andrew Lawson, MD

If you have an unwanted self of "stupid," then you will likely have a false self of "smart." If our unwanted self is that we *do not* want to be seen as "stupid," then we create a disconnection strategy of the false self that shows the world how "smart" we are, rather than being okay with looking "stupid" and connecting with our True Self.

We create these false selves because we believe our value is determined by what we accomplish or attain instead of who we truly are.

How to Figure Out What Our false selves Are

Our false selves are our brains attempt to protect us from others shaming us, making fun of us, if they were to see our unwanted selves. They are our persona's our masks our shields to protect us. Our outermost circle, false selves, are the masks we reveal to the world.

If our unwanted selves are a gaggle of scared, frightened little kids, then our false selves are a band of 'big brothers 'saying, "Hey kid get behind us; we will protect you."

For example, I called a cardiologist to consult on a patient in the emergency department and during the call the cardiologist asks why did you choose that medication to give the patient? This immediately sends me into my unwanted self circle and I can make a choice at this point. I can choose to embrace and follow the message of the unwanted self: "Hey Drew, he's calling you stupid, and he's telling you that you chose the wrong medication!" Which immediately takes me to my false self therefore responding by acting smart—responding to the cardiologist by being Spock and being all logic and all smarts. The other option is that I can make the other choice, if I'm aware of it, from unwanted self "he's calling you stupid" to True Self filled with curiosity and lifelong learning. A response that would look like me asking him to tell me more, teach me. The two options couldn't be more polarized: I wanna learn more versus the false self voice which might say to him, "I chose a beta blocker because clearly in the situation that is the smartest or correct medication to use."

Most of us have *no* idea that all this is going on in our brains, but our goal is to eventually develop the muscle of self-awareness to not only recognize this process but also to immediately pivot/shift this process so we can respond from our True Self and not our unwanted or false selves.

We are asleep to our unconscious motivations, and these motivations mask our True Self. In essence we are hiding. And the wound in our soul remains unhealed, infecting every aspect of our lives. We are so asleep to our reality that we don't know we are hiding behind the masks of our

Andrew Lawson, MD

There are, at the very least, three "big brothers" that enter the picture. If your unwanted selves is fear of failure, then a "big brother," who can be named "the controller,"[29] will likely be one of your false selves to try and control everything and prevent failure from showing up. If your unwanted selves is fear of being stupid (not enough, or incompetent), then a "big brother," who can be named "the protector,"[30] will likely be one of your false selves to try and protect/prevent/keep you safe and secure — anything to prevent you from looking stupid. If your unwanted selves is fear of being "unlovable," then a "big brother," who can also be called "the complier,"[31] will likely be one of your false selves to try and comply with everyone and prevent looking unlovable or unacceptable.

Our false selves speak to us...

You are ok if you act smarter than anyone in this room!

Just get along and they will like you

Show them that you are a success!

If my unwanted selves say I am unlovable, a failure, or stupid, then my false selves step in with an internal assumption that tells me I am just the opposite.

It is important to note that our false selves are the antithesis of our unwanted selves in the majority of cases. However, there are times in which we might have an unwanted self that has no opposite in our false selves circle and vice versa.

If in doubt, start by answering the question of the unwanted selves: "I would *die* if people thought I was ______________." Remember, our unwanted selves are the little, frightened kid, confused by the big world with an amygdala that is very active, trying to process whether he is safe or unsafe.

These primitive pathways start when we're little kids. The false selves are like a big brother, coming in front of our unwanted selves little kid and saying, "Get behind me. I got this." They shield and disconnects us from our unwanted selves and say, "Instead of failure, I'm going to be successful. Hear me roar. Instead of looking stupid, I'm going to look really smart." This is the dichotomy between the unwanted and false selves.

Just as our unwanted selves answer the statement: I do *not* want to be seen as ______________, our false selves answer the statement: I *do* want to be seen as ____________.

- I *want* to be seen as ______________.

- I will *survive* if people think I was ______________.

- I *want* people to think I'm ___________.

- I would *love* people to think I'm ___________.

These are the statements that our false selves answer, and as you can see, they are usually counter to our unwanted selves' statements and stories.

I want to be perceived as . . .

Here are some false self answers that others have said:
I want to be . . .

- competent

- intelligent

- enough

- in control

- reliable

- perfect

- hardworking

As we have discussed, when our amygdala gets turned on to fight, flight, or fawn, it turns on our false selves to control (fight), move against or protect (flight), or move away/toward to comply (befriend). We use all of these "shields,"[32] but we will have a dominant one that we use most often.

One of your false selves will be one of these three shields. You can now add your dominant shield false selves to your outer circle. You can personify it and develop a caricature of it. The more you associate your false selves with a funny person or creature, the easier it will be to separate yourself from its beliefs and behaviors, and the quicker you will respond to them when they show up.

The unwanted self known as the jerk and his big brother, false self Billy the Bully

Another unwanted self that we carry around with us in our brain chemistry is most commonly known as the "inner critic." But I call him "the jerk." We want to develop a caricature of this unwanted self.

This is our unwanted self that always tells you that you are "not enough." Many of us feel "not enough," and this drives the creation of the false self that can be known as Billy the Bully, who makes us try to look like we are enough. One of the ways it does this is by judging ourselves, others, and our circumstances.

The jerk unwanted self says to us, "You are *not* enough," while its big brother, Billy the Bully, says to us and to others, "Well, if I'm not enough, then you certainly can't be." This bully seeks out everyone and everything to make us feel enough, compared to everyone and everything else.

A few years ago, a new nurse was working with me. A patient who had overdosed on drugs came into room 5 in the emergency department where I was working. I immediately had to control his airway with a breathing tube. I was about to put the tube in when the patient started to vomit. The nurse was leaning over to clean up the vomit coming out of this patient's mouth and whispered to me, "This is bad, *really* bad." Afterward, I took her aside and said, "Please don't whisper like that while I am trying to intubate someone. I already had the voice of my "Billy the Bully" screaming in my head." We both laughed, although I am not sure whether she thought I was sane.

This false self that I have named "Billy the Bully" will be a bully to me and others, largely depending on my energy level. Think H.A.L.T.—Hungry, Angry, Lonely, and Tired. I tell my nurses and staff that if I get snarky during my final hour of my shift, "Billy the Bully" has shown up. Billy will judge, criticize, condemn, and complain about the actions of those around me, while my inner critic, the jerk, will focus on pointing out all the ways I am not enough.

> *This ceaseless voice is what literature professors call an unreliable narrator. . . . It will not shut up. . . . While we often accept the statements bubbling up from within this river of incessant chatter as being factual, most are actually a complex mixture of evaluations and judgments, intensified by our emotions. — Susan David, PhD*[33]

This false self bully is scanning our lives all day long saying, "This is bad." and "This sucks." It will say, "You suck," or "This sucks." In a famous old stallion story, the owner repeatedly says, "Who knows what is good and what is bad?" The jerk and Billy the Bully seem to know.

Again the key is personification, because as you play with unwanted and false selves, you recognize these voices, not as dark and gloomy and condemning, complaining, criticizing, and judging, but more as funny caricatures. You want to visualize your silly unwanted and false selves in a funny, silly way rather than in a large gremlin-type picture.

I have adapted these characteristics and information from the book: *Positive Intelligence* by Shirzad Chamine. The more we get clarity around our inner critic (The Jerk), the more we will recognize and play with he/she/it.

This is a process for you to develop the caricature of your Billy the Bully so you can add a picture of him/her/it to your outer, false selves', circle.

1. What does your Billy the Bully say to you?

2. How does your Billy the Bully' show up in your life and leadership?

3. What impact does your Billy the Bully' have on your decisions and influence?

4. Add a caricature of your Billy the Bully' to your false selves' circle, and also add a caricature of your inner critic, the Jerk, to your unwanted selves' circle.

The unwanted self bobby binary and his big brother false self, the judge.

Most of our unwanted selves develop when we are kids in response to the huge, often scary, world that we are trying to figure out. Our brains love to generalize and simplify our surroundings. This causes us to quickly label things as either good or bad. Touching a hot oven and burning our fingers is *bad*. Chocolate chip cookies are *good*. Our brains develop "bobby binary" to see the world only in good and bad or 1's or 0's.

This unwanted self whispers to us, "This is right," and "This is wrong," while his big-brother false self, the judge, points out to us and to the world why everyone and everything is wrong.

False selves' Online Test and their unwanted selves' little brothers

Another way to discover your false selves and their corresponding unwanted selves is to first discover your false selves and then discover their corresponding opposite "little brothers."

In Shirzad's Positive Intelligence work, he has created a brief online assessment (https://www.positiveintelligence.com/saboteurs/) that will give you insights into your dominant false selves or what he calls saboteurs. I have created a grid to help you recognize who might be your corresponding little brother (unwanted self) to your false self.

unwanted self message	false self
I do not want to be seen as imperfect.	stickler
I do not want to be seen as a failure.	hyper-achiever
I do not want to be seen as out of control.	controller
I do not want to be seen as displeasing, uncaring, unloveable, harsh, dogmatic, dictatorial.	pleaser
I do not want to be seen as a victim, lazy, apathetic.	hyper-vigilant
I do not want to be seen as dispassionate, lazy, uncaring, disconnected.	restless
I do not want to be seen as a trouble maker, disrupter, peace-killer, non-pleaser.	avoider
I do not want to be seen as stupid, not enough.	hyper-rational

How to recognize when our unwanted and false selves have shown up and some unwanted and false selves' factoids:

- All stress and anxiety

- Status quo

- Always want to be right

- Us versus them

- Make us think, feel, see narrowly

- Fear

- Negative emotions longer than ten seconds

This is a list of facts that can help us recognize, clarify, and know when our false selves are present.

In my coaching practice, I was taught some keys to knowing you are coaching a client's false selves instead of the actual client.

An unwanted or false self is in the room when . . .

- "Should on yourself"

- I can't . . .

- But . . .

- I need the other person to change

- This is the way it is . . .

- If I don't have or get __________, then__________

- Conversation feels like heavy lifting

Recognition of our false selves is over 90 percent of the journey.

false selves' Discovery

As we have now seen, we each have at least three false selves: The Judge, Billy the Bully, and one of the three shields.

Here are some questions to explore with your false selves' caricatures:

1. What are your false selves? Which one is dominant?

2. What does a bobblehead of your false selves (specifically, The Judge and Billy the Bully) look like? What would their fake IDs say?

3. What is its/her/his name?

4. What does it say to you?

5. When do you see it show up?

6. What emotions does it bring with it?

7. What is your posture when it takes charge?

8. How do you act when you listen to this false self?

9. What ways might this voice hold you back?

10. How would your life be different if you ignored this voice?

11. What can you do to prevent a false selves from showing up?

12. What can you do when a false selves shows up?

13. What can you do after a false selves shows up?

This chart is a summary of at least three of the major false selves and their corresponding unwanted selves.

false selves (Who I pretend to be.)	the judge (says,"this is all wrong!")	Billy the Bully' (says,"Everything and everyone is not enough!")	shields: controller (fight), protector (flight), complier (fawn)
unwanted selves (Who I don't want to be.)	bobby binary (says,"this is right. this is wrong.")	inner critic (says,"I am not enough!")	primitive fear responses: fight, flight, fawn

True Self

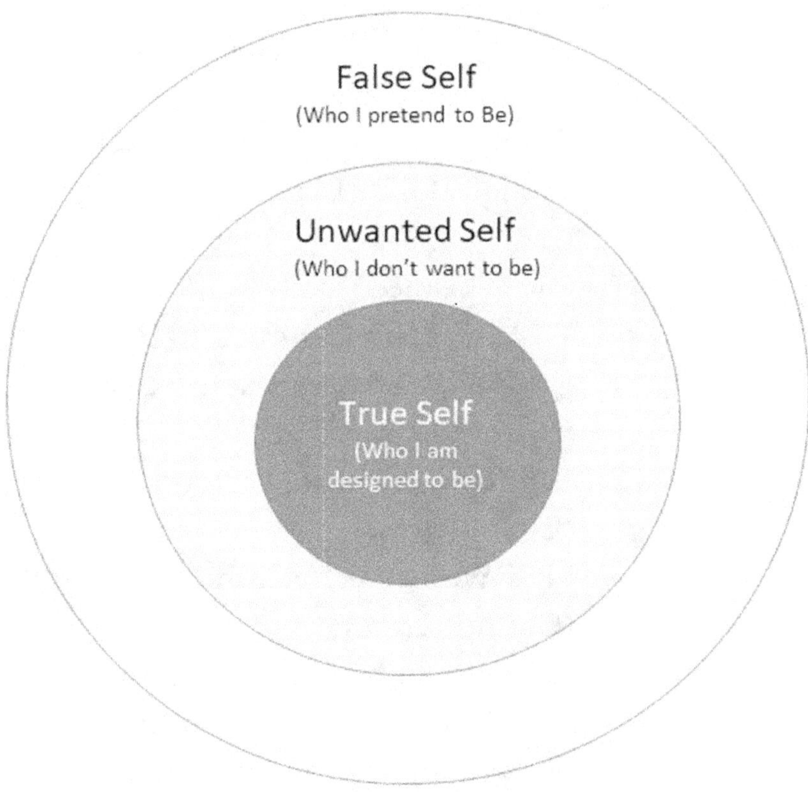

false self — Who I pretend to be.

1. Look Smart and Capable (Spock, The Tin Man, Answer Man)
2. I am enough (You are not enough) (Billy the Bully)
3. I am right/everything is wrong (The Judge)
4. Hard working/carry everything (Bag Boy/Backpack Man)

unwanted self — Who I don't want to be.

1. Stupid, incompetent, incapable, needy
2. Not enough (The Jerk)
3. Wrong (and everything must be right or wrong) (Bobby Binary)
4. Lazy
5. Overwhelmed (splat man)

True Self — Who I am designed to be.

1. **Curious, clueless, playful, quirky (Rosie the pug dog)**
2. **Intuitive, encourager, level 3 listener (Coach Drew)**
3. **NCRW, love & see others as God does (Caring Father)**
4. **Lean in, embrace, love tenderly, looks for "thin places" (Embracer)**
5. **Now here, abandon, whimsy, dance in the moment (Present Perfect)**

In the movie *Fred Claus*, a guy named Clyde is so angry and bitter that he tries to shut down Santa Claus and Christmas. In a powerful exchange between Santa Claus and Clyde, Santa remembers that Clyde had asked him for a Superman cape for Christmas many decades ago. Santa hadn't given it to him, because Clyde was on the naughty list that year. Santa pulls out a Superman cape and asks Clyde, now forty-five years old, to put it on. Clyde removes his glasses because Superman doesn't wear glasses, and Clyde goes on to work for Santa.

We all wear a superhero cape, our very own one-of-a-kind cape. This is our True Self.

> *There is something in every one of you that waits and listens for the sound of the genuine in yourself. It is the only true guide you will ever have. And if you cannot hear it, you will all of your life spend your days on the ends of strings that somebody else pulls.* — Howard Thurman[34]

We have lived our lives from the outside in. We have allowed people and circumstances to threaten our safety, identity, and worth rather than living from the inside out, connecting to our True Self.

You have now joined a rare, select few who know that our unwanted and false selves have covered up our True Self from us.

> *To excavate Essence (our True Self), we have to dig through a lot of mud. To unearth buried treasure, we have to get our hands dirty and dig deep into our soul. There's no other way to get there.* — Christopher Heuertz[35]

We have begun the work of digging through the mud of our unwanted and false selves, and now it is time to unearth our buried treasure, our True Self.

In *Star Wars: Episode VI — Return of the Jedi*, a powerful exchange between Darth Vader and Luke Skywalker reveals their relationship. Luke now knows that Darth Vader is his father.

Luke: "I've accepted the truth that you were once Anakin Skywalker."

Darth Vader: "That name no longer has any meaning to me."

Luke: "It is the name of your True Self. You've only forgotten. I know there's good in you. The emperor hasn't driven it from you. I feel the conflict within you. Let go of your hate."

Darth Vader: "It is too late for me, son."

Luke: "Then my father is truly dead."

Are you Darth Vader or Anakin Skywalker? Which do you want to be? What is holding you back?

For most of us, there is no conflict between our false selves and our True Self, because we live unaware that either one exists. But now we know, and we want to develop our awareness of our True Self so we can turn the volume up on our True Self and down on our unwanted and false selves.

Now we are going to focus on our True Self, our essence, or *soul* in some spiritual practices. It is the essence of who we are, our uniqueness.

The only true joy on earth is to escape from the prison of our own false selves, and enter by love into union with the Life Who dwells and sings within the essence of every creature and in the core of our own souls (True Self).
— Thomas Merton[36]

Our True Self is a diamond forged from years and years of high-pressure crushing of carbon. It is like no other diamond ever created, with unique cuts and qualities. Our True Self is a diamond. It is our essence. It is who God made us to be.

Finally, you look inside and see how God loves you just as you are, while still planning to make you the best possible version of who you are." *— Scott McKnight*[37]

Now that we are aware of all three of our circles, we have a choice when one of our unwanted selves shows up. We can either disconnect from our True Self and those around us by turning to our false selves (outer circle), or we can connect with our True Self (inner circle) and with others.

Connection Strategies

There are many connection (and disconnection) strategies. Here are just a few strategies to help us connect to our True Self.

Andrew Lawson, MD

The first connection strategy is to focus on self compassion. Professor Kristin Neff says there are three components to self compassion. The first being self-kindness: Are we treating ourselves, our True Self, as we would treat someone we love? Do we see our unwanted and false selves like our favorite quirky high school teacher? The second component to self compassion is common humanity. This is recognizing and normalizing that we ALL struggle with self compassion. The third component to self compassion is mindfulness. Dr. Neff has a great self assessment that can help each of us better understand how self compassionate we are with ourselves. (https://self-compassion.org/self-compassion-test/)

A third connection strategy is a practice known as Loving Kindness in which you meditate on these phrases:

- May I allow myself to be imperfect.

- May I accept myself just as I am.

- May I trust that I am enough right now.

- May I remember that there are people who care about me.

A fourth connection strategy is to discover our values. This process is known as Values Clarification:

Intimacy, beauty, authenticity, freedom, loyalty, learning, adventure, faith, magic, connection, risk taking, inspiration, trust, mastery, fairness, courage, thoughtfulness, competition, patience, growth, self-reliance, contribution, clarity, balance, solitude, health, resilience, nature, uniqueness, autonomy, purity, elegance, collaboration, community, harmony, openness, free spirit, focus, directness . . . The list goes on and on.

This is a list of values. You will hear the terms convictions and values being used interchangeably. I am okay with that. I see *convictions* as corporate, stodgy, and "shoulds," whereas I see *values* as a word or phrase that *grabs* you and *calls* to you when you read it.

Many people will say I'm trustworthy, and that could be a value of mine. But it could be a characteristic of who I am. When people say, "Oh, Drew's really trustworthy," I take that as a compliment, but that's not compelling to me. Trustworthiness does not pull itself from the page and come alive, and therefore, it is not one of my values.

Go through this homework exercise, read the words, and look for the words that excite you, that really speak to you, that you believe are unique to who you are—not necessarily words that equate to what people say you are or what you think are important because someone said you have that character quality.

1. Select your "top 10" values from the list. Pick out the words that really resonate with you. When you are doing or feeling this word, you feel most

alive. (note: you may add values/words that you don't see listed or are not captured the way you prefer)

2. Rank them in order of importance.

3. Rate on a 1-10 scale how successfully each value is showing up in your life now.

Values Ranking	Values Rating (from 1-10)
1.	
2.	
3.	
4.	
5.	
6.	
7.	
8.	
9.	
10.	

Intimacy	Beauty/Aesthetics	Authenticity
Freedom	Loyalty	Learning
Adventure	Faith/Spirituality	Magic

Connection	Recognition/Affirmation	Risk Taking
Creativity	Inspiration	Trust
Achievement	Mastery/Excellence	Service
Fairness	Compassion	Integrity
Courage	Thoughtfulness	Competition
Patience	Personal Growth	Self-Reliance
Responsibility	Honesty	Contribution
Clarity	Balance	Solitude
Zest	Performance	Legacy
Health	Resilience	Nature
Vitality	Romance	Dependability
Uniqueness	Autonomy	Altruism
Purity	Elegance	Collaboration
Partnership	Self-Expression	Community
Orderliness/Accuracy	Harmony	Openness
Nurturing/Mentoring	Free Spirit	Freedom to Choose
Lack of Pretense	Focus	Directness

Andrew Lawson, MD

Please see endnotes for further exercises to help you discover your values.[38]

- faith/belovedness
- family/devotion/loyalty
- inspiration/magic/miracle
- connection/collaboration/transparency/authenticity
- curiosity/creativity/learner/ideas/wonder
- zest/perseverance/challenger

This is an accumulation over the years of words and phrases that remind me of who I truly am. Some of them are strengths. Some of them may be characteristics, but ideally there is a listing for all of us that we can use to focus on our values.

The words grouped with backslashes (for example, faith/belovedness and family/devotion/loyalty) are called value streams. As you develop your True Self values list, you'll see words and phrases that seem to be linked together in a common theme. Some of these words won't make sense to people, such as floppy-eared pug dog/quirky/humor, but that is okay. These values and their streams are for you. They are for you to clarify and connect with your True Self.

Eventually these value streams will lead to personifications or caricatures embedded within our True Self, just like we have caricatures embedded in our unwanted and false selves (for example, Spock and The Jerk).

In my coaching practice, I use the behavior assessment called DiSC. There are many assessments out there: Myers-Briggs, SDI, etc. Many of us have taken these assessments, but have we ever thought of them as a tool to shed light on our True Self? Dig up any assessment that you have taken, grab a highlighter, and highlight the words and phrases that call out to you when you read them. Ah, that truly represents part of my uniqueness, my True Self."[39]

My Inside Team (aka Board Room)

True Self

Caring Father	• Sees everyone as NCRW
	• Sees others as God sees them
	• Loves others as God does
Embrace	• Lean In
	• Embrace
	• Love Tenderly
	• Looks for "thin places"

Coach Drew	<ul><li>Intuitive</li><li>Encourager</li><li>Level 3 Listener</li><li>Asker of powerful questions</li><li>Blurter</li><li>Deepen the learning</li><li>Curious & clueless</li><li>Flip the switches up on all I encounter</li></ul>
Rosie the Pug	<ul><li>Curious</li><li>Clueless</li><li>Playful</li><li>Quirky</li></ul>
Playful	<ul><li>Confident</li><li>Mischievous (Calvin)</li><li>Ready for Action</li><li>More than Enough</li></ul>
Present Perfect	<ul><li>Now Here (vs Nowhere)</li><li>Quirky pug dog humor</li><li>Laugh more—myself and others</li><li>Abandon, whimsy, love</li><li>Dance in this moment</li></ul>

Purpose	<ul><li>Catalyzing & developing emotionally intelligent leaders and their systems to be better, more efficient, more productive, more sustainable, more resilient, and more fulfilling</li><li>Joining men on their journeys to know their brokenness and recognize and embrace their belovedness</li></ul>

First we explore and discover our unique values, then we link common values together into value streams, and finally we create caricatures that embody these value streams. These characters make up what some call a "board room" or "inside team" that makes up our True Self inner circle.

This is a schematic of my "inside team."

This begins the process of creating neurochemical pathways that initially compete and eventually override the old, embedded neuropathways of our unwanted and false selves.

Just like we use the caricatures of our unwanted and false selves to clarify and play with, and more easily recognize the voices of our unwanted and false selves, we can also use these caricatures to tap into our True Self more easily. For example, if I want to utilize the attributes of Coach Drew in a meeting, I will connect with the values that are within my Coach Drew identity. I will go to the meeting as Coach Drew, filled with curiosity and great listening. For time with my kids, I might want to embrace Caring Father attributes. By doing this, I have more clarity around my superpowers, my characters who create my True Self, and I will certainly make better decisions.

One of your homework assignments will be to develop your "inside team," taking clusters of values that you've started to think about and then personifying them into characters.

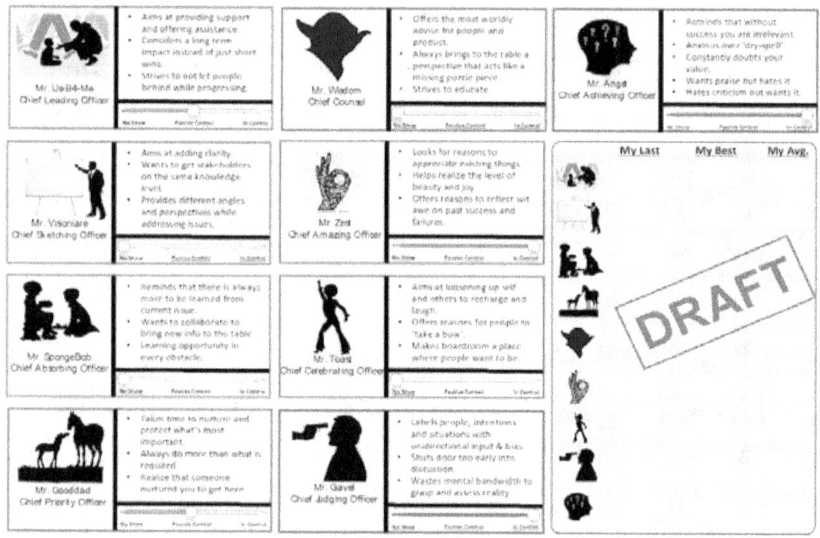

This is another example of an "inside team" or "board room" that one of my clients created, which also included unwanted and false selves' characters that technically need to be located in the outer circles.

- What are the values of your True Self?

- When does your True Self show up?

- What impact does your True Self have on your influence and decision making?

Begin development of your inside team (aka boardroom).

Bringing It All Together

In this chapter we will look at a few more concepts and some exercises for individuals and teams. I think it's helpful in a team and in one-on-ones to start with the question about unwanted selves, because it's a very emotionally charged and usually a more readily accessible statement to answer: I would die if people thought I was ______________.

Remember if our unwanted selves are our little, scared kid, and the big brother to that kid would be our false selves that come up and say, "Hey, get behind me, I got this," then this big-brother false selves become our shield or mask, our outward appearance to the world. They try to protect the unwanted selves as well as disconnect us from our True Self. It answers the statement: I would love people to see me as ____________. It will usually be the opposite to our unwanted selves.

Outside In versus Inside Out

The vast majority of us are living our lives from outside in. We are living with the belief that our safety, identity, and worth come from our unwanted and false selves' circles. This allows the outside world of people and circumstances to always threaten our safety, identity, and worth. We see and interpret everything through our unwanted and false selves' lenses, and they are interpreting everything we see and hear as a message screaming at us from the outside world: "I am not enough. I am not smart enough. I am not successful enough. I am not lovable enough." This creates a constant sense of insecurity, sense of fear, sense of not being enough, and sense of feeling unsafe. This is why it is so important to continue this journey, to shift from a sense of insecurity, confused identity (an identity given to us from the outside world), and unworthiness to one of a constant sense of safety and True Self identity and inherent worthiness.

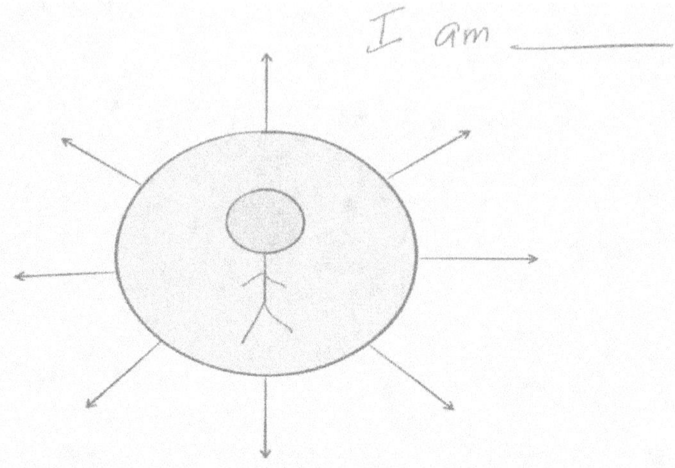

If we can function from inside out, we function from our True Self, confident in who we are, confident in our identity and worthiness. When we live from our True Self, our safety, identity, and worth can never be threatened, because we are embracing the truth that we are a designed, unique diamond, and we know the unique essence of who we are.

If we can live in this place, then fear is replaced by love. Insecurity is replaced by security. And confusion of our identity is replaced with clarity of our identity. Our sense of unworthiness is replaced with a sense of worth. This is why it is so important to understand and get clarity around our True Self.

Compare & Contrast True Self and false selves

false self	True Self
• Fear	• Open
• Arms crossed	• Arms open wide
• Contracted	• Curiosity
• Judgment	• Hope
• Shame	• Spacious
• Scarcity	• Lightness
• Restricted	• Stillness
• Heaviness	• Enoughness
• Restless	
• Not enough	

An exercise that I've done with clients and their teams is taking a piece of paper and putting two columns, one for True Self, one for unwanted selves or false selves.

I'm reminded of a client whose dominant false selves' shield was a controller that he had embedded into his neurochemistry. We did this exercise in his home while I was staring at a life-size photograph of him in his college football uniform. As he was struggling to get clarity around what this controller looked like, I said to him, "Who's that over there?" It immediately dawned on him that this picture of him in his football stance was a representation of his controller. He walked over to the picture frame, lifted it off the wall, and put it in the closet, which is such a great example of the awareness of the controller in him and in all of us.

For the True Self, you can put your name or the name of one of your inside team members. For the false selves, you can put down one of your false selves. Next, think about the attributes for each of these, and you will quickly recognize how different they are and how they're clearly defined.

True Self taps into our trust network of our brain, which is fueled by oxytocin and produces:

- Patience

- Compassion

- Positivity

- Optimism

- Calm

- Gratitude

- Curiosity

false selves tap into our fear and distrust network of our brain, which is fueled by cortisol and produces:

- Frustration

- Anger

- Negativity

- Pessimism

- Impatient

- Resentment

- Judging

Other questions that you can ask:

1. What do you notice about these 2 lists?

2. What can you do to shift yourself to your True Self list?

3. How can you prevent yourself from getting stuck in your false selves' list?

You will see that I listed physical postures on both lists—arms crossed and arms open wide. In executive-coach training, they use the term *geography* for the use of physical gestures, which is a great way to connect us to our brain chemistry as well as provide a physical reminder of whether we are in True Self mode or false selves' mode.

I had a client who knew his hyper-rational false self was taking over the meeting when his hand reached for his glasses to put them at the end of his nose. A great early warning system.

This activity can be done generically or with specific false selves of the client as well as with teams. What's the team's True Self look like? What are the team's collective True Self attributes? What are the team's false selves' messages?

There are many different ways to parse this, but it is a really great exercise to work with individuals or with teams.

	Habitual Views	Lead to intentions	Create experiences of ...
false selves	• Win / Lose	→ To attack / demand	Fear, anxiety
	• Right / Wrong	→ To protect / defend	Anger, aggression
	• Conflict is dangerous	→ To blame / judge	Shutting down, freezing
	... a problem, gone wrong		Judgment, rejection
	• Others as objects	→ To coerce / manipulate /	Disconnection
	in relation to our needs	control	Alienation

	Skillful Views	Lead to skillful intentions	Create experiences of ...
True Self	• Win / Win	→ To inquire / listen	Intimacy, safety
	• Conflict is natural	→ To care	Belonging
	... a ground for learning	→ To collaborate	Understanding
	• We share universal needs	→ To connect	Mutual respect
	• Inherent value in others		Creativity, synergy

This is an excerpt from a great book on communication: *Say What You Mean* by Oren Jay Sofer. In this graphic, he talks about two pathways for intentional speech and intentional communication. One of them is this habitual intention that starts with right and wrong. Conflict is dangerous, which then leads to an intention of attacking, protecting, and blaming, which creates this experience of fear and anxiety. This sounds familiar, right? When I saw this framework, I thought, *This describes our false selves.* The habitual views leading to certain intentions, which leads to experiences of a false selves or a True Self view of "win-win" and "conflict is natural." It's a learning opportunity. This leads to great intentions of care, collaboration, connection, listening, and in turn leads to experiences of intimacy, safety, belonging, and understanding. This is really a great chart to illustrate the impact of our false selves or our True Self can have on our community and ourselves.

Using your three selves' circles with two people and a conflict

Here is another activity geared specifically for teams. The individuals on the team have done a values discovery exercise where they each came up with two of their individual values, and then lead them through a discovery session to help them understand their unwanted and false selves. You then ask for two volunteers, and using paper tape, make two large circles abutting each other.

Have the two volunteers pick a topic that is contentious with the group, a topic that they've had issues with. Have them both stand in the false selves outer circle so they are standing right next to each other.

As we have learned, the posture from the false selves is filled with blame, shame, disapproval, and tension. Their individual postures and speech will likely be trying to "fix" the conflict.

Have them take a time-out and step into their True Self circle, asking them what two values that they chose. Now have them discuss the topic that was just "debated," but this time coming from the True Self inner circles.

You will find it really incredible to see the shift in their voices, their postures, their tone, and what they are saying to each other. This is a powerful exercise to illustrate what we've learned and also how we can individually and collectively make a difference by using these techniques.

Questions to use for this exercise:

1. What is a recent conflict that you have been in at work or home?

2. Reenact this conflict with your partner from one of your false selves.

    - What do you notice?

    - Did the conflict arise due to a false selves' involvement?

    - What impact did your false selves have on your influence and decision making?

3. Reenact this conflict with your partner from your True Self.

    - What do you notice?

- What effect did your True Self have on this conflict?

- What impact did your True Self have on your influence and decision making?

4. What did you learn when you had a conflict from your false selves' circle?

5. What did you learn when you had a conflict from your True Self circle?

Using three selves' circles with your team

This is another team activity. It's looking at the three circles in the context of your team in two ways: The first way is looking at how your team thinks it is seen by the outside world. The second way is looking at how your team sees itself.

These exercises can be done with the team leader to help them to better understand their team, or they can be done with the entire team to help the team better understand team dynamics.

How do others see your team?

How do you think your team is perceived by the outside world, starting first with: What's the unwanted itself? Answering the sentence: Your team does not want to be perceived as ______________ by the outside world. Responding to this sentence leads to an understanding of the teams' false selves.

Andrew Lawson, MD

Looking at your team in the context of these three circles, how does your team think it is seen by the outside world (outside in or externally)?

How do they "not want to be perceived as" from the outside world (unwanted self/team)?

Example #1: How others see your team

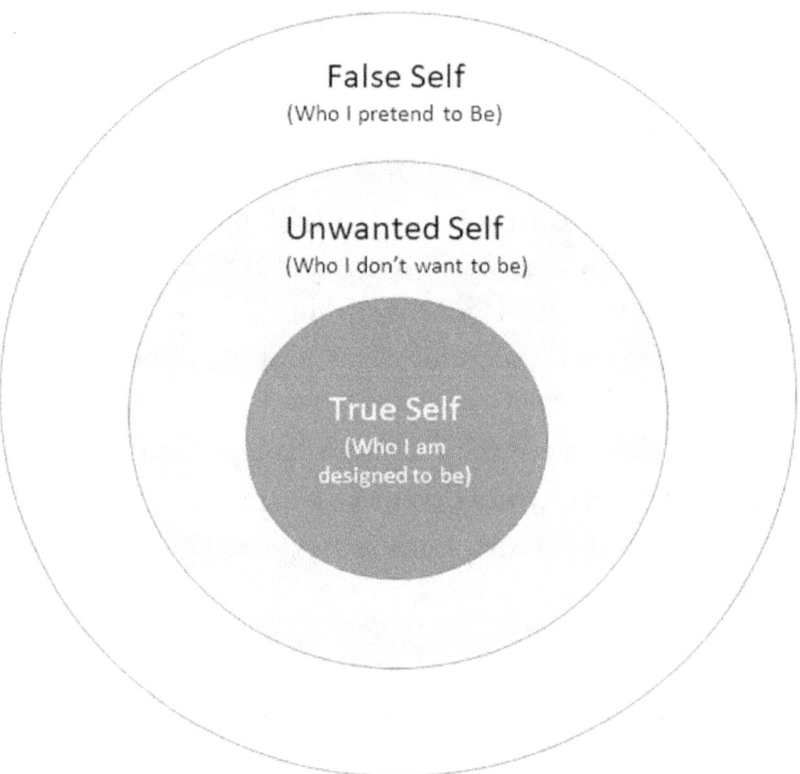

false self — Who I pretend to be.

- Experts in everything

unwanted self — Who I don't want to be.

- Service Provider

True Self — Who I am designed to be.

- Strategic Partner

This is an example from one of my clients. This is how his team thinks others see them (externally—from outside in).

These are the questions:

1. How does the rest of the company see your team?
   From the unwanted selves' perspective: Service Provider.

1. How does the rest of the company see the team from the false selves' perspective?
   Answer: Experts in Everything.

2. How does the team want the rest of the company to see them?
   Answer: Strategic Partner.

Clearly, very powerful insights, very helpful to go over and to absorb with the team.

Example #2: How others see your team

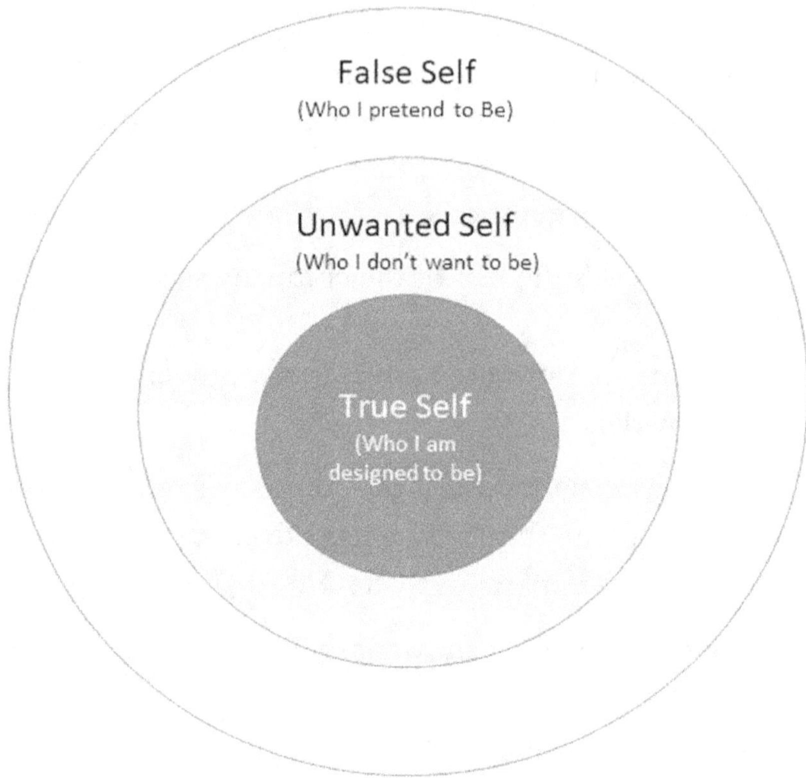

false self — Who I pretend to be.

- Reliable

unwanted self — Who I don't want to be.

- Unreliable

True Self — Who I am designed to be.

- Calm, Prepared, Controlled, Confident

This is another example of how this team thinks they are perceived by the rest of the company from the perspective of each of the circles.

How does your team see itself?

Ask your team collectively to fill in the blank of the unwanted selves' statement. Take the dominant answer.

1. How does the team answer the unwanted selves' statement we/I do not want to be seen others as

   _____________.

   Likely answers: weak, lazy, stupid.

2. The team members' false selves will be the opposite to their unwanted selves.
   Answer: strong, hardworking, smart. This is how each team member wants to be seen by their teammates.

3. Next find the opposite of your team's dominant answer and create a funny caricature of that false self.

4. Additionally, you can have each individual discover two of their values and pick one or two of their combined dominant values to create a funny caricature of that dominant value to go into the teams True Self inner circle. You might end up with "Baby Yoda" in the True Self inner circle and a body builder caricature in the false selves' outer circle.

From this information, you can empower the team to be more aware and give them the ability to shift their decisions from predominantly false selves to True Self (Baby Yoda likely makes much better decisions).

Example #1: How your team sees itself

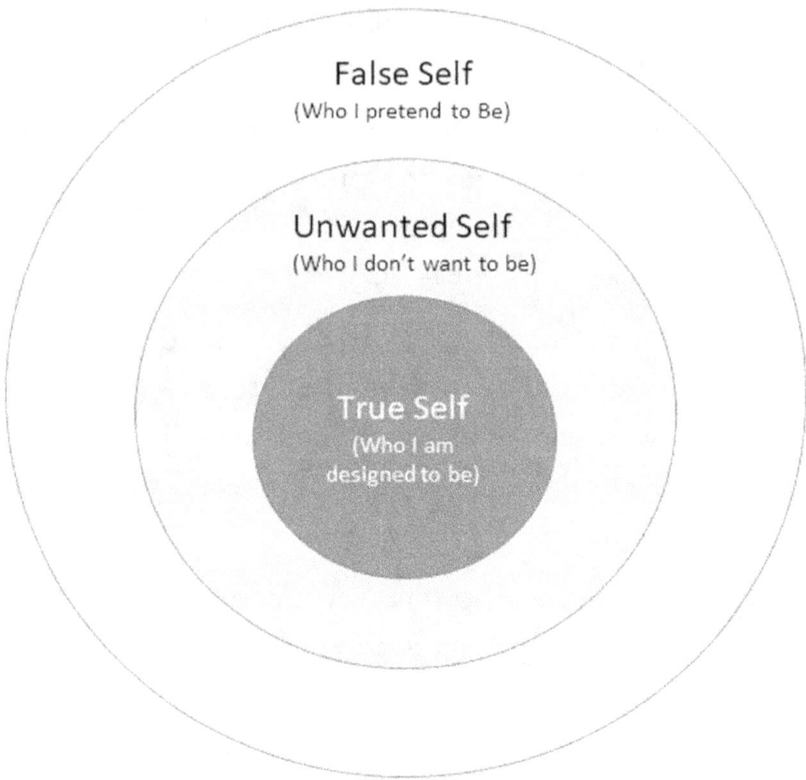

false self — Who I pretend to be.

- Strong, Capable, Hardworking

unwanted self — Who I don't want to be.

- Needy, Lazy, Need to be Pushed

True Self — Who I am designed to be.

- Open, Honest, Hive

In this example I asked the client, "What's the message embedded in their unwanted selves?"

He said, "The theme for this year that came out was that they really did not want to be seen as needy, lazy, or needing to be pushed."

So then I asked, "What does that look like? What's the false self that covers that up for them?" Answer: strong, capable, and hardworking. This manifests itself by not wanting or being willing to ask other teammates for help, and so they carry around the sense that they've got it all covered. They're hardworking and capable and strong. God forbid that they would ever have to ask someone in their team that they need help. This clearly makes the team less successful.

Then I asked him, "What do you want the True Self to be at the core of your team?" Answer: open and honest and like a beehive that is constantly in communication, constantly connected with one another and constantly helping one another out. A beautiful illustration of the power of this tool in a team dynamic setting with a team leader.

Example #2: How your team sees itself

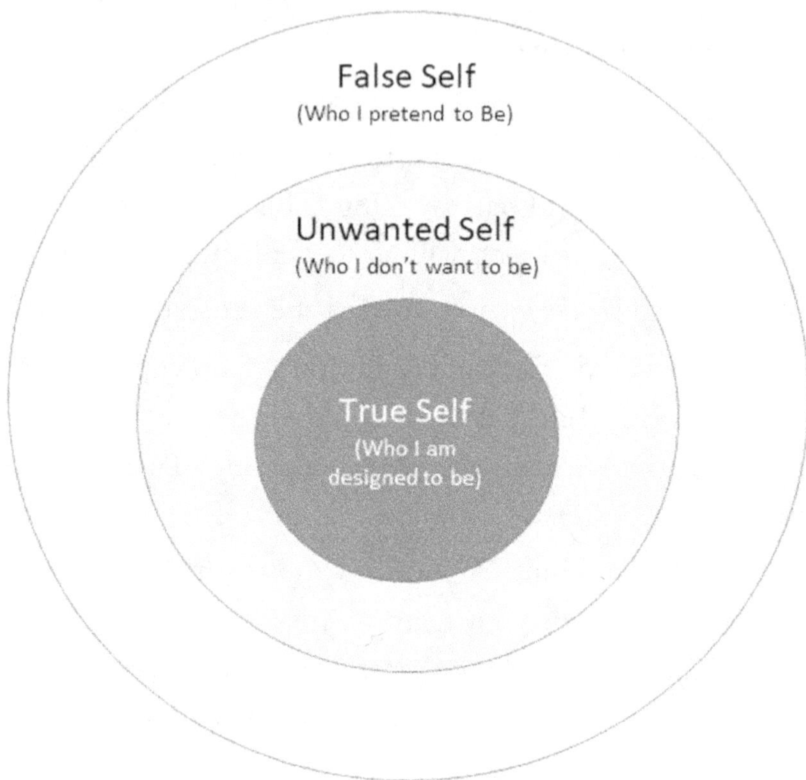

false self — Who I pretend to be.

- Good Enough, Looking Good

unwanted self — Who I don't want to be.

- Not Good Enough

True Self — Who I am designed to be.

- Getting Better, Celebrating Failure

Individual and/or team beliefs and behaviors linked to their three selves' circles

	Belief	Behavior
FALSE selves		
UNWANTED selves		
TRUE SELF		

This grid can be another exercise to get more clarity on our three selves and their underlying beliefs and behaviors.

For example, one of my partners hadn't seen me in a while, because I haven't been working as many shifts this year due to COVID. I showed up for a shift, and he jokingly said, "I thought you didn't work here anymore. I haven't seen you in so long."

Kind of a zinger, right? As I thought about that, I applied it to this grid. Starting with unwanted selves, which is always a great place to start, I realized that it was a zinger to me because my unwanted selves said, "You have been working less, so you are weak and lazy." This is the belief that can drive either a connection or disconnection. Driving to disconnection is creating a false self of "look and work hard" to protect my unwanted self of weak and lazy, thereby disconnecting my True Self from the rest of the world.

Andrew Lawson, MD

So my belief around one of my false selves would be that working harder than anyone else would give me safety, identity, and worth. My behavior would then be very little sick days, never taking a sick day, even when I'm really feeling horrible. In fact, I still work in a faster, harder-than-anyone-else mode. I'm constantly moving. Looking at my True Self of "present perfect" reminds me that the belief that all we have is the present moment, so don't miss it by working frantically and missing out.

The behavior I manifest when I'm in that True Self space is slowing down, being mindful, and connecting with others. This is helpful when working on my relationships with my coworkers and with my patients. Clearly a True Self belief and behavior—embedding that into my interaction with my partner and my interaction with others—is very important.

	Belief	Behavior
FALSE selves	Working harder than anyone else gives you safety, identity, worth.	Two sick days in 25 years. Working faster and harder than anyone else.

UNWANTED selves	Working less is weak and lazy, and you are a loser. Your partner is calling you "weak and lazy."	
TRUE SELF	Present Perfect: all we have is the present, so don't let it go by working feverishly and missing it.	Slowing down and being mindful and connecting with others.

For homework, pick one of your false selves that is linked to one of your unwanted selves. Also establish a True Self value stream or value, and answer the following questions:

1. What True Self beliefs help you? Why?

2. How can you turn the volume up on these beliefs?

3. What True Self behaviors help you? Why?

4. How can you turn the volume up on these behaviors?

5. What false selves' beliefs hold you back? Why?

6. How can you turn down the volume on these beliefs?

7. What false selves' behaviors hold you back? Why?

8. How can you turn down the volume on these behaviors?

Conclusions

There is no fear in love. But perfect love drives out fear.
— 1 John 4:18

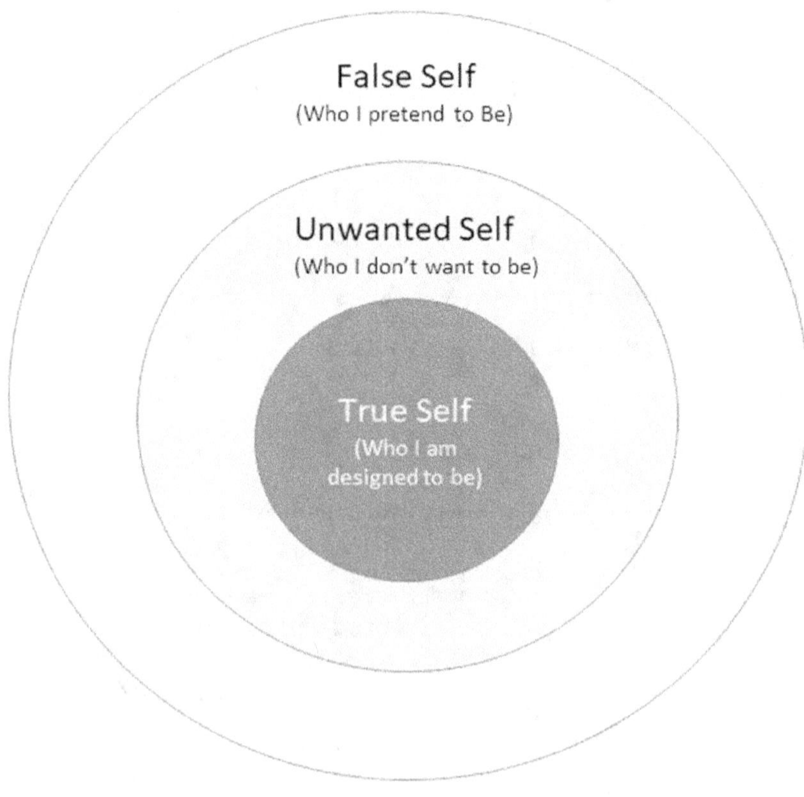

false self — Who I pretend to be.

- FEAR

unwanted self — Who I don't want to be.

- FEAR

True Self — Who I am designed to be.

- LOVE

Our True Self is inherently love-based, and it's designed by a Creator for us to be focused on our uniqueness and our design to be love-driven leaders. Our unwanted and false selves are fear-driven, and clearly lead to unsuccessful, fear-driven decisions.

Remember, our ultimate goal will be to have two circles. Our True Self circle being very large and highly developed and our unwanted selves' circle being paper thin and translucent to the world. It has been shown that vulnerability is a *key* leadership quality. We must live with our unwanted selves. They are our brokenness. We must "wear" our brokenness on our "sleeves." Our unwanted, broken parts are the key to our connectedness—to ourselves and others.

He paused again so his emotions could catch up to him, momentarily knocking the wind out of his speech. For a time he seemed to be staring at a piece of his story that only he could see.

"I wore three T-shirts," he finally said, swallowing back his tears, "well into my adult years, cuz I was ashamed of my wounds. I didn't want no one to see 'em." Then he suddenly found a higher perch upon which to rest.

Andrew Lawson, MD

We must be willing, vulnerable, and able to share our unwanted selves to the world. Until we lean into our brokenness/our unwanted selves and are willing and able to be vulnerable with others about our brokeness/unwanted selves, we will remain tethered to our false selves.

The embrace of our own suffering helps us to land on a spiritual intimacy with ourselves and others. For if we don't welcome our own wounds, we will be tempted to despise the wounded. — Greg Boyle[41]

Our inner circle of True Self shines like the unique diamond that it is, with its one-of-a-kind cut, color, and glimmer and its unique flaws (unwanted selves) for all the world to see.

Like a diamond with rough edges and hairline fractures, you'll realize how even seemingly unattractive parts of yourself make you not only who you are, but are crucial to the unique beauty that is you. — Christopher Heuertz[42]

There is a crack in everything, that's how the light gets in.—Leonard Cohen

Getting rid of our false selves to have our True Self and unwanted selves remain is the ultimate pathway to our belovedness and our brokenness. We are looking constantly to connect versus disconnect. I think the unwanted and false selves in us, specifically the false selves, are disconnection strategies. We have a choice to make when we have the unwanted selves within us get triggered. We make a choice to either (1) connect and choose to go toward our True Self and connect with the other person and be vulnerable and acknowledge our unwanted selves or (2) we choose to disconnect, which leads us to our false selves, the big brothers that try to protect us and end up disconnecting us. I think the ultimate journey for all of us is to eliminate the false selves' circle and live with the rawness and vulnerability of our unwanted selves, being our skin, being the part of us that's exposed to the world. This may well be the tougher journey, but it's a journey of brokenness and connectivity, which ultimately leads us to connect with our True Self and our belovedness.

I am reminded of the lotus and the mud story. The lotus (our True Self) is *part* of the mud (our unwanted selves), and without the mud, the lotus cannot bloom.

A lotus has its roots in mud. It rises through muddy water until it pierces the surface and blossoms as a gorgeous flower that delights all who see it. The lotus represents the beauty and purity of our fundamental nature (our True Self). And what about that sucky, yucky mud? That

Andrew Lawson, MD

Final discovery exercises #1

One exercise that I would love all of us to develop is the
$9.99 yearly theme bracelet. At the end of each year, I
review my journal and summarize all that has happened
that year. I then look for a theme or mantra for the new
year. Once I arrive on a theme or mantra, I order a
$9.99 bracelet with the theme emboldened on it. The
funny thing is that the theme I often pick is one of my
many unwanted selves. Cluless (purposely misspelled)
was my theme bracelet last year. It is a very transparent,
vulnerable reminder of my brokenness that I display to
myself and the world. My clients have joined in at times,
either choosing an attribute of their True Self or one of
their unwanted selves.

This is a homework challenge for you. What is your theme bracelet going to say? Is it one of your True Self values? Or one of your unwanted selves?

I know from experience that wearing one of my misspelled unwanted selves on my sleeve for a year made for some fun and thought-provoking conversations. And it reminded me of my brokenness and helped me build my vulnerability muscles.

Final discovery exercises #2

false self — Who I pretend to be.

1. Look Smart and Capable (Spock & The Tin
    Man-Others: clueless, sappy, naive; life is
    about logic, reason, being smart, being
    intelligent; belief: task over relationship,

thinking not feeling; Triggers: when people are emotional; Emotions: to show emotions is weakness, if I feel then I will be exposed as weak, unreliable, vulnerable & Answer Man-Expert, consultant, "sit down, shut up, & listen")

2. I am enough (You are not enough) (Billy the Bully)

3. I am right/everything is wrong (The Judge)

4. hard working/carry everything (Bag Boy/Backpack man)

unwanted self — Who I don't want to be.

1. stupid, incompetent, incapable, needy, "cluless"

2. not enough (The Jerk) Others are: clueless, confused, stupid, weak, lazy, needy; Belief: you are not enough; Emotions: fear, anger, anxiety, stress; EAS syndrome: External Affirmation Syndrome; elder son

3. wrong (and everything must be right or wrong) (Bobby Binary)

4. lazy

5. splat man (The world is going to end; I am going to die. overwhelm, worrier.)

6. "Loston"-You are totally lost; you will never find your way

7. foolish-You look foolish; you act foolish; you are an embarrassment.

True Self — Who I am designed to be.

- Rosie the pug dog: Curious, clueless, playful, quirky

- Coach Drew: intuitive, encourager, level 3 listener, asker of powerful questions, blurter, deepen the learning, curious & clueless, holder of space (Chap Quote)

- Caring Father: sees everyone as NCRW, love & see others as God does

- Embrace: lean in, embrace, love tenderly, looks for "thin places"

- Present Perfect: Now here (vs nowhere), laugh MORE-myself and make others laugh, abandon, whimsy, love, dance in this moment (Steven king poem)

- I am playful, confident, mischievous (Calvin), ready for action, and MORE than enough!

The final product and what this might look like for you. I'm hoping by now that you have some of this filled out.

A Toolkit to Help Manage Our Three Selves[44]

This chapter provides us with tools, insights, and tactics that have been shown to help us manage our Three Selves.

What is the most complex object in the universe?

Answer: The Brain

- 1.1 trillion cells

- 500 trillion microprocessors wired together

- billions of synapses activated every second

- uses 25 percent of the body's oxygen and glucose stores[45]

The brain is made up of trillions of cells. It's got microprocessors, trillions of them, all wired together, and billions of synapses, which are the places where the neurons connect and talk to each other. And they're activated, billions of them, every second.

About 25 percent of all of our energy stores are used by this tofu substance like brain that's sitting on top of our necks. Our brains have a couple things going on.

Malleability

First, the brain is malleable and neuroplastic. Back in the 1980s and 1990s when I was in training, the belief was that after a certain age, your brain wasn't able to be malleable. It couldn't be rewired or do different things. But now we've learned that it can. For the rest of your life, you can retrain your brain, and your brain has the plasticity—or the malleability—to change.

We want to recognize the wiring and know how to rewire and strengthen, and in some cases, weaken our neural connections. Just like a supercomputer, bandwidth is key. The thicker the insulation around the wiring, the faster the connection.

Take learning how to ride a bike, initially, there's just a few little neuron connections talking together. But as you ride a bike more and more, your brain develops thick sheaths around the neurons needed to coordinate bike riding. The more you practice, the thicker the sheaths (known as myelin) around the neurons that have wired together to allow you to ride a bike. The more frequently used pathways get thicker and faster.

What we want to do is use our ability to retrain the brain and recognize those pathways to help us to be better leaders.

Laziness

The Brain is lazy so it creates stories. Our brain is lazy because it knows it has a limited supply of glucose. When it sees somebody who looks a certain way and sees another person who looks similar, it makes the "lazy" connection that they are the same, when in reality, they are very different. It's stingy in the way it uses its resources. And that's what creates stories.

We know from research that eyewitness testimony is notoriously inaccurate. And we know that what truly happened in our childhood is foggy to us. If we had a video to watch scenes from our childhood, that video would be very different from the story that is embedded in the neural networks of our brains.

In our neural pathways, we have these embedded stories, that our brain has made up. Our brain takes these little fragments and puts them together to make stories, and it makes them very simple. To save and conserve its energy, our lazy brain might say, "Oh yeah, that thought looks like that one, so these are the same." That's where we get into trouble. Recognizing these fundamental traits of the brain will help us as we go forward.

Over time, we develop stories in our head, and we develop these thought processes like "I am bad," or "I'm a failure," and the more we think unwanted and false selves' thoughts, the more our brain makes these connections wire strong and fast. If you make a bad choice or something doesn't go right at work, that neural connection pathway is *so* strong and fast that you immediately think, "I'm a failure."

Of note, when the brain is put to use to think and think hard, it can drain us of a tremendous amount of energy. My undergraduate faculty advisor, Robert Sapolsky, who studies stress in primates at Stanford University, says a chess player can burn up to 6,000 calories a day while playing in a tournament, three times what an average person consumes in a day. Sapolsky suggests that grandmasters' stress responses to chess are on par with what elite athletes experience.[46]

RAS to the Rescue

Finally, it is important to remember that our brain—specifically its Reticular Activating System (RAS)[47]—focuses on what is most important, and we can set our RAS to focus on the positive True Self. We can choose what our brain focuses on. However, most of us are on autopilot and allow our RAS to focus on the negative unwanted and false selves.[48]

The Toolkit

I am now going to discuss some key components to help us. They will also help us be more playful in this process of facilitating our brain's neuroplasticity.

These are ten tools to help us wire, unwire, and rewire our brain chemistry.

#1 Play and Personify

We are *not* our unwanted and false selves (remember to identify, play, and personify them). For example, as I mentioned earlier, I have a false self that I call "Spock."

One of the most effective ways to manage our unwanted and false selves is simply to observe and label these thought patterns as soon as you notice them. It is important that we separate our True Self from these other selves as we take this adventure on—and do it with laughter and a playful attitude.

This is illustrated by UCLA professor of psychiatry Dr Swartz's breakthrough with the children he was treating with OCD. He created some simple steps in their therapy, the most important of which was the realization that they were *not* their OCD. Their OCD was a "brain freeze"—a rut in their synaptic pathways of their brain. He had the children with OCD in his study remember to tell themselves, "I am not my OCD."

When we talk about all these different false and unwanted selves wired into our brain chemistry, we want to be careful of the language as we go along. We don't want to say, "Oh, that's part of me," or "That's me." No, no, no. We want to say, "John has a false self that says X, Y, and Z." We want to realize that's the brain pathway that's causing the thought process that's causing this voice that talks to you in your head. It is separate from us. It is a chemical pathway in our brains, and it is not who you truly are. Therefore, we're going to be mindful about recognizing that. In Swartz's research, he found that this was a key mantra to help these kids rewire their synapses.

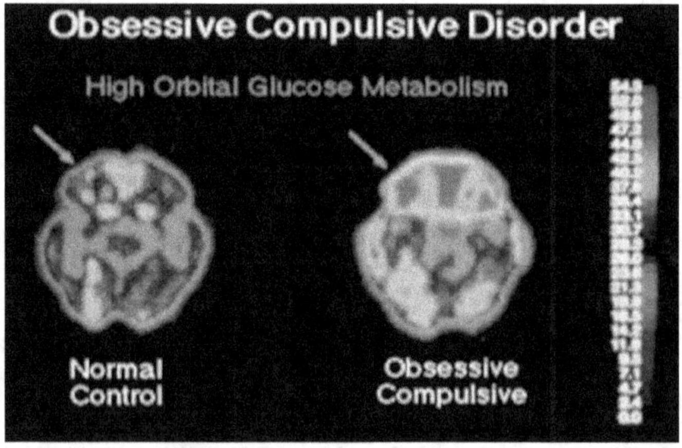

In this image, we see a PET scan of a child with OCD on the right. After six months of therapy using the concept that "I am *not* my OCD," these children were able to rewire their synapses to look like a normal brain without OCD (the image on the left). This is profound. This means we can indeed rewire our brains.

My son has OCD. During his formative years, he was a very good tennis player, but his OCD would get in his way. He called balls *in* that were clearly *out*, because his OCD told him to. To counteract this, he placed a crumpled-up piece of paper on the bench next to his tennis bag to personify his OCD. He told this piece of paper that represented his OCD, "Hey, OCD. Just sit and watch me play tennis and don't get involved."

Again, remember that we are *not* our unwanted selves nor our false selves.

Three other points need to be made. The first is to remember to laugh and play with these unwanted and false selves' neural pathways. We must remember that they are simply a cluster of neurons that are making up these thought patterns. The second key point is that the more we can personify these unwanted and false selves (creating personalized descriptions and names for them), the easier they are to recognize and manage.

One of my unwanted selves, I have named "the jerk" based on the funny character from an old Steve Martin movie of that name. Having a picture, or better yet, a bobble head on my desk of "the jerk" makes me laugh and smile when I hear the jerk's silly comments in my head.

Finally let's face it. Most of us spend the majority of our lives inside our heads—thinking and ruminating over our many racing thoughts. We hear our thoughts as voices talking to us. We all have voices in our heads. This is part of having an advanced neocortex. One study says that we can talk to ourselves at up to 1,000 words per minute!

Ethan Kross, author of the book *Chatter*, points out that these voices are best managed when we are intentional about placing them into the third person.[49] When one of our thoughts registers in us as "I am SO stupid." It is best to designate that voice as one of our unwanted selves' characters and translate it to "splat man" (yes one of my many unwanted selves) just said to me, "Hey Lawson, you're going to lose everything."

Research shows that we ruminate less, have less negative emotions, and can even improve our performance by switching to self talk in the third person using the name of one of our unwanted selves. This is further evidence that naming and personifying the voices in our heads is so important.[50]

#2 Mindfulness

Mindfulness is the second tool in the wiring/rewiring toolbox. It allows our brains to be more flexible, to pivot more quickly, and to calm the unwanted and false selves neural pathways that cause us to get stuck.

In Shirzad Chamine's book *Positive Intelligence*, he emphasizes that mindfulness and meditation are the two most important practices to manage our unwanted and false selves. One of his recommendations is easy and transformative. It is to do what he calls Positive Quotient (PQ) reps throughout the day. Each of these mindfulness reps is like a rep you would do while lifting weights. Each rep adds to your mindfulness "muscles." A single rep involves shifting as much of your attention as you can to your body and/or any of your five senses for at least three seconds. He recommends doing 100 reps per day, or approximately fifteen minutes per day, of these mindfulness reps. As you develop your mindfulness "muscles," your brain will be less "stuck" on your unwanted and false selves' neural pathways.

One of the simplest ways to get your reps in is to connect them to daily routines. When was the last time you stopped and were fully present to feel the toothbrush run across every individual tooth? When was the last time you took a shower and listened to the sound that it makes, when you felt the temperature of the water and acknowledged the water rolling over your body? When was the last time you walked your dog and were fully present to see the trees and all the things that were around you? When you exercise, when you eat, when you listen to music, when you're hanging out with loved ones—how often are you mindful about being fully present with them?

Finally, some of the best opportunities to do reps are when you notice an unwanted or false self showing up. You can use these selves as personal trainers to get your reps in.

Building Your Mindfulness Muscles: Breathing & Vision

There are two unique and direct ways to turn off your fight or flight responses and get your mindfulness reps in:

The first is breathing. Breathing is a voluntary and involuntary activity. When we use tactical or box breathing, we directly switch off our fight-or-flight responses and quiet the voices of our unwanted and false selves. I have gotten in many reps during the peak of the COVID pandemic by doing what they call box or tactical breathing while wearing a respirator in the emergency department. Box breathing is simply inhaling for a count of four, then another count of four at the height of inhaling, then a count of four as you exhale, and a final count of four at the end of your exhale. Doing this box breathing for two to four rounds immediately calms your system and quiets any unwanted or false selves' voices.

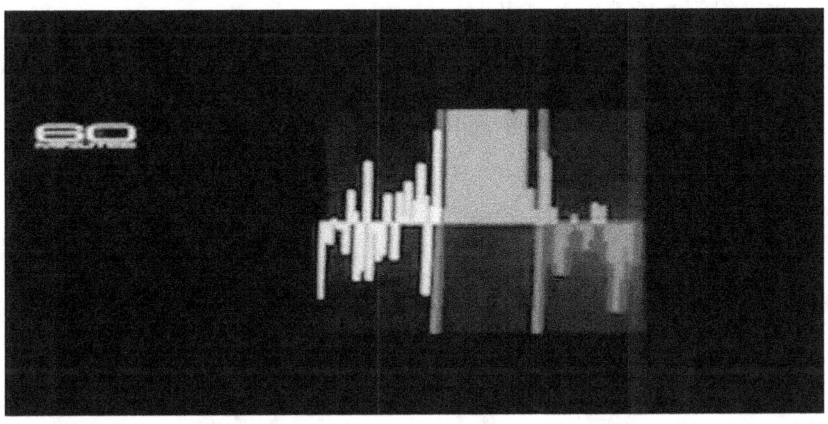

In fact, Anderson Cooper did a special for *60 Minutes* on mindfulness. This is a picture of Anderson's brain activity. As he thought of something traumatic the spikes went red and high, but at the moment when he was asked to use a mindful breathing technique, his brain wave activity immediately calmed.

The second way is your vision.[51] Your eyes are part of your brain. They are a direct extension of your brain. In fight-or-flight mode, or when the voices of our unwanted and false selves show up, your vision tunnels.

Andrew Lawson, MD

If you look at the horizon, pull up to big views, panoramas, the sky, and sunsets, you are shutting down your fight-or-flight response and those pesky voices.

#3 Meditation

All human evil comes from this: our inability to sit still in a chair for half an hour. — Blaise Pascal

Another essential tool to manage our unwanted and false selves is meditation.

I have found it to be a game changer. If you don't buy into it, that's okay. I didn't. It took reading half a dozen books before I started to warm up to it, but now I'm a big believer in it. I firmly believe it changes your brain chemistry, and there's a lot of new research showing support for that. If you want to have this self-directed facilitated neuroplasticity and really be able to wire your brain the way you want it, meditation is going to be a key component of that in your life.

I've noticed over the years since I've been regularly meditating that my stress response still occurs, but instead of it going up high and then very slowly recovering back to baseline, I have found that I get the stress response and then very shortly afterward go back to normal—much more quickly than I used to. It's important to recognize the power and importance of meditation. I encourage you all to try meditation using the Headspace app for thirty days.

#4 Be Curious and Nonjudgmental

Curiosity is the antidote to judgment.

This is my Rosie, the pug dog who is always curious. "Be like Rosie," I tell others. After teaching some of this content in the hospital, one of our charge nurses came up to me and said, "Dr. Lawson, I went pug on that doctor the other day." Initially being very worried about that, I asked her, "What does that mean?" She said, "An OB/GYN doctor in Room 3 came in and started throwing instruments because she couldn't find what she needed. I walked in as the charge nurse, and I just turned my head like a pug dog. I opened my hands up to her, and I just said, 'Hi, I've never met you. Who are you? How can I help you?'" The doctor responded in a positive way, despite all the chaos. The power of being a curious pug dog will go a long way in this process for you.

Curiosity and judgment cannot live in the same room together. And the story that best illustrates the power of nonjudgment goes like this:

The Stallion Story

When an old farmer's stallion wins a prize at a country show, his neighbor calls round to congratulate him, but the old farmer says, "Who knows what is good and what is bad?" The next day some thieves come and steal his valuable animal. His neighbor comes to commiserate with him, but the old man replies, "Who knows what is good and what is bad?" A few days later the spirited stallion escapes from the thieves and joins a herd of wild mares, leading them back to the farm. The neighbor calls to share the farmer's joy, but the farmer says, "Who knows what is good and what is bad?" The following day, while trying to break in one of the wild mares, the farmer's son is thrown and fractures just like. The neighbor calls to share the farmer's sorrow, but the old man's attitude remains the same as before. The following week the army passes by, forcibly conscripting soldiers for a war, but they do not take the farmer's son, because he cannot walk. The neighbor thinks to himself, "Who knows what is good and what is bad?" and realizes that the old farmer must be Taoist sage. — From the Tao Book and Card Pack by Timothy Freke

I am guessing that we all can think of a situation that we labeled "bad" that later turned out to be an incredible opportunity or gift.

Our unwanted and false selves will tell us, "Of course we know what is good and bad." They are very rigid and judgment oriented. But the reality is that we really don't know what is good or bad. Who really knows what the future of the boy in the story could be? So be nonjudgmental. Don't hold tightly to your unwanted and false selves' preconceived ideas.

#5 Your Safety, Identity, and Worth

Find where your safety, identity, and worth are located:

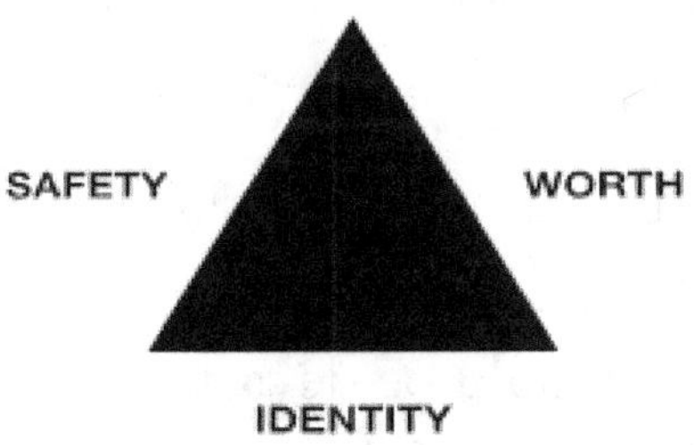

Where do your safety, identity, and worth come from? Do they come from your True Self, unwanted selves, or false selves?

Be mindful of where this triangle of safety, identity, and worth is located, because if these are tied to our false selves, we will be highly reactive and ugly.

However, when these are tied to our True Self, we can make empowered choices.

> *True emotional safety is not dependent on how others treat us. It is based on how we understand and relate to our own experience, on our own sense of [safety, worth, and identity].* — *Oren Jay Sofer*[52]

When you look at the three circles, we want you to ask yourself, "Is this little triangle embedded in our false selves' circle?" For example, if somebody attacks our outer circle, our false selves, then we're going to rear up and say, "Oh my gosh, they're telling me I am unsafe, unworthy, and without an identity other than the one the person is giving me." Or does this triangle fall into your True Self circle?

I had a client say that if I, his coach, would say to him, "You are a failure," that he would be devastated. I reminded him that, "You may fail at things, but you are never a failure." I asked him to see where his triangle was located. If he would be devastated by someone telling him that he was a failure, then his triangle was likely in his false selves' or unwanted selves' circles. If he realizes that he is never a failure, but he does fail at things sometimes, then his triangle is located in his True Self circle.

We want to journey toward getting the triangle of identity, worth, and safety embedded into our True Self circle, because that's where all our true safety, identity, and worth come from. If we can get to that place where we can trust and believe in that and know that, then amazing things can happen.

#6 Prepare

Shirzad also talks about what he calls a "preemptive strike" in his book, *Positive Intelligence*. A preemptive strike is the super skill of preparing and anticipating what false and unwanted selves to expect to show up *before* they do.

There are three skill levels in managing our unwanted and false selves.

- Level 1: recognizing when they show up after the event that triggered them.

- Level 2: recognizing them as they are showing up.

- Level 3: preparing for them before they show up.

The most advanced skill level is recognizing the situation that is about to happen and preparing yourself for the unwanted or false selves before they show up.

#7 Turn Up the Volume

We need to turn up the volume of our True Self by focusing on our purpose and vision.

Our unwanted and false selves cannot be in the same room when the volume is turned up on our True Self, which contains our purpose and vision.

#8 H.A.L.T.

We want to avoid trying to manage our unwanted and false selves when we are Hungry, Angry, Lonely, and/or Tired.

#9 Bobbleheads, Fake IDs, and Wanted Posters

The key to playing with your unwanted and false selves is to create caricatures of them (for example: the Spock). I always challenge my coaching clients to imagine, or better yet, *create* a bobblehead[53] of each unwanted and false self to put on their desk for them to see all the time.

It doesn't have to be a bobblehead, but I want the caricature you develop to be light, fun, and visible so you are being reminded daily of its presence.

Another option is to develop a fake ID for each of your "fake" selves.

#10 Rewriting the false self stories in our head using Non-Violent Communication principles

Another strategy comes from the principles of Nonviolent Communication (NVC):

When we have a judgmental dialogue going on within, we become alienated from what we are needing and cannot then act to meet those needs. — Marshall B. Rosenberg, PhD[54]

In Dr. Rosenberg's book, he describes a woman who shared that she had two false selves vying for her attention:

false self #1—Career Woman: "I should do something more with my life. I'm wasting my education and talents."

false self #2—Responsible Mother: "I'm being unrealistic. I'm a mother of two children and can't handle that responsibility, so how can I handle anything else?"

Dr. Rosenberg asked the woman to restate each of these false selves' messages using the NVC format: "When A, I feel B, because I am needing C. Therefore, I now would like D."

Her translation went like this:

false self #1—Career Woman: "*When* I spend as much time at home with the children as I do, without practicing my profession, *I feel* depressed and discouraged *because I am needing* the fulfillment I once had in my profession. *Therefore, I now would like* to find parttime work in my profession."

false selfs #2—Responsible Mother: "*When* I imagine going to work, *I feel* scared *because I'm needing* reassurance that the children will be well taken care of. *Therefore, I now would like* to plan how to provide high-

Andrew Lawson, MD

quality childcare while I work and how to find sufficient time to be with the children when I am not tired."[55]

What kind of day/life will you choose to have?

About the Author

Drew's dynamic leadership background and work history has transformed the lives of many.

He has master's level advanced executive and physician coach training matriculating through rigorous certification processes to provide his clients with cutting-edge coaching and team facilitation. With extensive experience in removing barriers to success and using practical and proven methods to improve efficiency and productivity, Drew helps his clients boost profitability and job satisfaction.

As a practicing emergency physician at a major trauma & medical center in Southern California, a senior partner in his emergency medicine group, and former quality assurance director, Drew continues to lead teams through crisis-driven, high-conflict, and stressful work environments. Through applied coaching techniques, his never-crack-under-pressure demeanor and strong leadership abilities, Drew continues to transform the culture of his team to improve service quality, workplace communication, and customer satisfaction.

By combining his passion for teaching, mentoring, and coaching with his experience in the chaotic world of Emergency Medicine, Drew helps business leaders and healthcare providers minimize their blind spots, improve communication and conflict management skills, cast powerful visions, and master their leadership abilities.

Drew earned his Bachelor of Science degree from Stanford University, where he was a scholarship athlete, and his Doctor of Medicine from Jefferson Medical College, where he was an academic scholar. He returned to Stanford for his emergency medicine residency. In addition to his education in medicine, Drew holds a number of coaching credentials including: Board Certification, Professional Certified Coach, Leadership Circle 360 Certified, Strengths Deployment Inventory Certified, ORSC (Organizational Relationship Systems Coach) Certified, Brené Brown's Daring Way Certification, and Certified Physician Development Coach. As a coach, consultant, strategist, and speaker, Drew continually equips others to reduce conflict, build teams, and drive results.

Drew lives in Newport Beach with his high school sweetheart. He has three adult children with whom he loves spending time. His family and friends speak often of his curiosity, enthusiasm, authenticity, wisdom, and quirky humor. Outside of work, Drew holds true to his lifelong passions for learning and fitness as an avid reader and swimmer.

Endnotes

1 Excerpt from Barking in the Choir by Greg Boyle

2 Excerpt from Barking in the Choir by Gregory Boyle

3 Chatter by Ethan Kross pg 64

4 Excerpt from The Pause Principle by Kevin Cashman

5 Lama, Dalai, tutu, Desmond. The Book of Joy, page 31

6 Heuerts, Christopher. The Enneagram of Belonging, pg 19

7 The Emotionally Healthy Leader: How Transforming Your Inner Life Will Deeply Transform Your Church, Team, and the World

8 Lama, Dalai, Tutu, Desmond. The Book of Joy, page 14

9 Chamine, Shirzad. Positive Intelligence: Why Only 20% of Teams and Individuals Achieve Their True Potential AND HOW YOU CAN ACHIEVE YOURS (p. 152). Greenleaf Book Group Press. Kindle Edition.

10 Ferguson et al. Unwanted Identities: A Key Variable in Shame—Anger Links and Gender Differences in Shame; Sex Roles, Vol. 42, Nos. 3/4, 2000 and Brown, Brené. I Thought It Was Just Me (but it isn't) (p. 82). Penguin Publishing Group. Kindle Edition.

11 Heuertz, Christopher L. The Enneagram of Belonging
https://books.apple.com/us/book/the-enneagram-of-belonging/id1488274654

[12] Carl Jung, "Psychology and Religion" (1938). In CW 11: Psychology and Religion: West and East, pg 140

[13] Carl Jung, "Good and Evil in Analytical Psychology" (1959). In CW 10. Civilization in Transition, pg 87

[14] Christopher Heuertz, The Enneagram of Belonging, pg 176

[15] *Although many of us think of ourselves as thinking creatures that feel, biologically we are feeling creatures that think. — Jill Bolte Taylor*

[16] *Nouwen suggested we all find ourselves bouncing around three very human lies that we believe about our identity (3 main unwanted selves, one of which we each have as a dominant unwanted selves): I am what I have, I am what I do, and I am what other people say or think about me.* — Heuertz, Christopher L. The Sacred Enneagram (p. 20). Zondervan. Kindle Edition.

[17] *Keating explains that as children we all need an appropriate amount of power and control, affection and esteem, and security and survival for healthy psychological grounding. But as we mature, our tendency is to over identify with one of these programs for happiness, keeping us developmentally and spiritually stuck.* — Heuertz, Christopher L.. The Sacred Enneagram (p. 22). Zondervan. Kindle Edition.

[18] Tim Ferris interview on Unlocking Us Podcast with Brené Brown, December 2020

[19] Emotional Agility, pg 18

[20] *Your brain reconstructs bits and pieces of past experience as your neurons pass electrochemical information back and forth…your brain combines information from outside and inside your head to produce everything you see, hear, smell, taste, and feel . . . your brain actively constructs your experiences. . . . neuroscientists like to say that your day-to-day experience is a carefully controlled hallucination . . . ultimately constructed by your brain.* — Lisa Feldman Barrett, PhD. *7 1/2 Lessons About The Brain,* page 65

[21] Brown, Brené. I thought It Was Just Me (but it isn't) (pp.73-74)

[22] Our brains average seventy-two thoughts per second.

[23] *We allow ourselves to get hooked by our emotions . . . when we get hooked . . . we start to go a little unconscious . . . (with meditation & mindfulness) . . . when things start to get bad now, I perk up. When I become aware that I'm closing down, I actually get a little excited. Here is a chance to reverse the old pattern and pull myself up! — Pema Chodron*

[24] *As an aside, if you are like me. I have had a hard time getting clarity around what the exact emotion that I am experiencing. A great app to help with this is by a Yale Professor, Marc Brackett, PhD. The app is called: MoodMeter.*

[25] Sofer, Oren Jay. Say What You Mean (p. 82). Shambhala. Kindle Edition.

[26] Chodron, Pema, Welcoming the Unwelcome

[27]

Primitive Brain Responses

	FIGHT	FLIGHT	BEFRIEND
Horney	go against	go away	go towards
Fear (UNWANTED SELVES)	Failure, worthless, insignificant	Stupid, incompetent, incapable	Unloved, imperfect, separated
Keating	power & control	security & survival	affection & esteem
Nouwen	"I am what I do"	"I am what I have"	"I am what others say about me"
DISC	D	C	I
Enneagram	1, 3, 8	5, 6, 7	2, 4?, 9

This graphic is my attempt to 'onnect the dots from a list of sources to help us better understand all the links that create our dominant unwanted selves.

[28] Heuertz, Christopher L.. The Sacred Enneagram (pp. 31-32). Zondervan. Kindle Edition.

[29] Anderson, Robert J., Adams, William A. Mastering Leadership. Wiley. Kindle Edition

[30] Anderson, Robert J., Adams, William A. Mastering Leadership. Wiley. Kindle Edition

[31] Anderson, Robert J., Adams, William A. Mastering Leadership. Wiley. Kindle Edition

[32] The terms: control, protect, comply come from the research found in the book: *Mastering Leadership* and the shield term comes from the work of Brené Brown and the Stone Center at Wellesley

The Reactive Tendencies

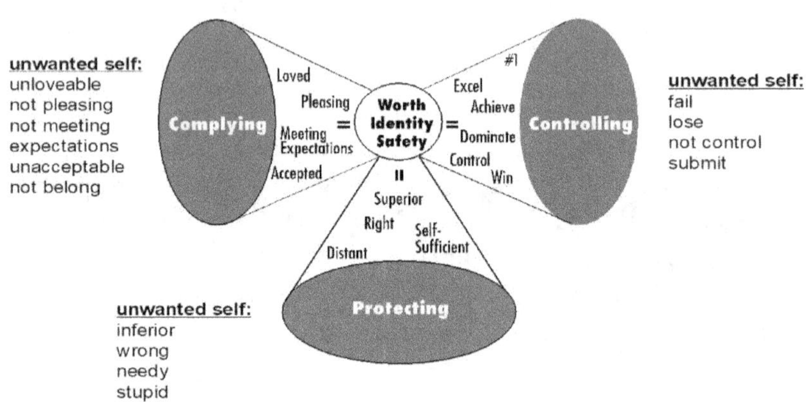

Reactive Tendencies is a term derived from adult developmental psychology and the research of The Leadership Circle 360, which points out that 75 percent of the population are "stuck" in this reactive space. This group of individuals (in which we are *all* a part of) believe that their safety, identity, and worth are linked to what people think about them. Each reactive tendency is linked to the three stress responses: fight, flight, and befriend. Each of these "shields" have unwanted selves linked to them. You will also notice words and phrases that are the beliefs linked to each of the shields.

It all goes back to the bunny rabbit. Everything in our outside environment comes into our amygdalae and asks the unsafe-or-safe question. If unsafe, then our sympathetic nervous system goes wild. We release epinephrin, we release cortisol, and we are ready for one of three things: We are ready to fight, which is this controlling posture that you see on the right. We are ready for flight, which is this protecting posture. Or we are ready to befriend, which is the comply posture. Comply, control, or protect are the three-shield false selves that our brains are wired to use in response to "Unsafe! Unsafe! Unsafe!"

If my brain is on autopilot and hears the "Do you even work here anymore? '"comment, my unwanted and false selves will automatically fire up, interpreting such a comment as a threat to my identity, safety, and worth. Then my protector shield shows up.

In my case, my protector, the Spock-like character in my false selves circle will come out. He will act smart, distant, self-sufficient, and superior. Again, I'm letting the outside world, my partner in this case, determine that my worth, identity, and safety come from him rather than from within myself.

Someone else with a comply shield will have unwanted selves of unlovable, not meeting expectations, unacceptable, or not belonging. Then the comply shield comes in and looks and acts lovable and pleasing and meeting expectations, trying to get along and be accepted.

[33] David, Susan, *Emotional Agility*, pg 20

[34] Howard Thurman, baccalaureate address at Spelman College on May 4, 1980

[35] Christopher L Heuertz. "The Enneagram of Belonging." Apple Books. (Pg 169) https://books.apple.com/us/book/the-enneagram-of-belonging/id1488274654

[36] Thomas Merton. "New Seeds of Contemplation.", pg 25.

[37] Excerpt from Scott McKnight interview:
https://www.christianitytoday.com/scot-mcknight/2020/november/interview-trevin-wax.html

[38] ## Values & Fulfillment

Too many people die with their music still in them. — Justice Oliver Wendell Holmes

What is your own special music?

What fills you up? What nourishes you? What gets your blood pumping? When are you most alive? What's really important to you?

What do you value?

We all have values that create resonance in our lives-values that excite us. The first step in our process together will be to better isolate/create a list of values that resonate for you.

Once we find out what we value, we will be able to more accurately prioritize our lives and achieve work and life fulfillment.

For example, a value of mine might look like humor/zany/Calvin(of Calvin & Hobbes)/Rosie. This is a value chain of mine. (note: Your value chain, like mine, doesn't have to make sense to anyone but you.) Rosie is my pug dog and she ALWAYS makes me laugh and smile because she is funny, goofy looking, and full of energy. Although funny looking is not a value of mine, Rosie is because I value laughter and energy. We hope to create some value chains like this for your life.

These Value Questions will help us to develop your values list. Have fun creating and exploring your answers. I would consider reading over and thinking about these questions for a few days before you compose your responses.

Let me know if you have any questions

Values Exercise #1: Peak Experience

Describe a peak experience (a powerful life changing event in your life):

what are you doing?

Who are you with?

What are you feeling?

Why was this experience so important to you?
Which of your values show up in this peak experience?

Values Exercise #2: Suppressed Values

What makes us angry, frustrated or upset is often something
that is contrary to a high value. In other words, it's a value that is
being suppressed. The experiences that most upset us are clues to
values that are being suppressed. For example, getting stuck in
commuter traffic frustrates you. You become antsy and angry. If
someone were to ask you what makes you so angry in that
situation, you might reply "I have no control, I'm trapped." The
opposite of loss of control and feeling trapped would be a
glimpse of what you really value i.e. Being in control and/or
being free.

What drives you crazy?

Values Exercise #3: Must Haves

Beyond food, shelter, and community, what are the needs
that you must have in your life to feel fulfilled? Example:
Adventure? Partnership? Accomplishment?

What accomplishments do you think you must occur during
your lifetime so that you will consider your life to have been
satisfying and well lived—a life of few or no regrets?

Values Exercise #4: Secret Passion

If there were a secret passion in your life, what would it be?

If time and resources were not a concern, describe the things
you long to do.

What's missing in your life, the presence of which would have
your life be more fulfilling?

What activities have heart and meaning for you?

Values Exercise #5: Obsessive Expression

We all are capable of obsessive behavior—insisting on honoring a value as a demand. For example, everything must be in its place to the point of perfection. When we insist on something—my way or the highway—there is a good chance there is a value being expressed in the extreme. What feedback do you get from friends and family? For example, if you often hear: "You are so controlling. You hog all the attention." These statements might point to a value of leadership or recognition.

Are there any places in your life where you may be taking a value to the extreme?

Values Exercise #6: Interview Questions

Ask 3 or 4 family members, friends or colleagues to answer these questions about you. Write down what you hear them saying and ask yourself: What values are reflected in their answers to your questions?

If I were on the cover of a magazine, what magazine would it be, and what would the story be about?

What do you see as my special talent or gift? What do I do naturally and effortlessly that is special?

When am I most fully expressing this gift or talent?

Family, Friend, or Colleague:	#1	#2	#3	#4
Cover of Which Magazine?				
What is the Story?				
My special gift or effortless talent?				

When am I expressing this gift or talent?				
What are my Values reflected in their answers?				

<u>Values Exercise #7: Values Ranking</u>

1. Select your "top 10" values from the list. Pick out the words that really resonate with you. When you are doing or feeling this word, you feel most alive. (note: you may add values/words that you don't see listed or are not captured the way you prefer)
2. Rank them in order of importance.
3. Rate on a 1-10 scale how successfully each value is showing up in your life now.

Values Ranking	Values Rating (from 1-10)
1.	
2.	
3.	
4.	
5.	
6.	
7.	
8.	
9.	

10.	

Intimacy	Beauty/Aesthetics	Authenticity
Freedom	Loyalty	Learning
Adventure	Faith/Spirituality	Magic
Connection	Recognition/Affirmation	Risk Taking
Creativity	Inspiration	Trust
Achievement	Mastery/Excellence	Service
Fairness	Compassion	Integrity
Courage	Thoughtfulness	Competition
Patience	Personal Growth	Self-Reliance
Responsibility	Honesty	Contribution
Clarity	Balance	Solitude
Zest	Performance	Legacy
Health	Resilience	Nature
Vitality	Romance	Dependability
Uniqueness	Autonomy	Altruism
Purity	Elegance	Collaboration
Partnership	Self-Expression	Community
Orderliness/Accuracy	Harmony	Openness
Nurturing/Mentoring	Free Spirit	Freedom to Choose

Lack of Pretense	Focus	Directness

As we gain more clarity about your values, your values serve as guideposts on your journey. You will then have the tools to ask important questions such as: "Will this decision honor my values?" and "What values will I honor by choosing A or B?"

(Portions adapted from: The Coaches Institute, Talane Miedaner, & The Gaillour Group)

[39] This is a Wordle. This one was created by my daughter when she was youngster. I want you to create your own Wordle. A Wordle is a collage of words that describe who you are at your essence, your True Self. It is a listing of adjectives and phrases describing your essence filling up to capacity, your True Self space.

[40] Excerpt from Greg Boyle's *Barking to the Choir*

[41] Excerpt from Greg Boyle's *Barking to the Choir*

[42] Christopher Heuertz. The Enneagram of Belonging. Pg 18

[43] Pema Chodron. Welcoming the Unwelcome.

[44] Landsberg, Max. Mastering Coaching: Practical insights for developing high performance. Profile Books. Kindle Edition.

[45] https://www.rickhanson.net/the-science-of-positive-brain-change/

[46] "Grandmasters sustain elevated blood pressure for hours in the range found in competitive marathon runners," he says. https://www.espn.com/espn/story/%5C_/id/27593253/why-grandmasters-magnus-carlsen-fabiano-caruana-lose-weight-playing-chess

[47] https://www.youtube.com/watch?v=QCnfAzAIhVw

[48] *If we are going to coach effectively, then we will need to facilitate change in some of that circuitry. Indeed American psychiatrist and leading researcher into the brain's flexibility Jeffrey Schwartz has defined coaching as "facilitating self-directed neuroplasticity.* — Landsberg, Max. Mastering Coaching: Practical insights for developing high performance. Profile Books. Kindle Edition.

[49] *Chatter* by Ethan Kross, pg 72–73

[50] Known as *illeason* after Julius Caesar's use of third person in his writings. See pg 72–73 in *Chatter* by Ethan Kross.

[51] https://www.scientificamerican.com/article/vision-and-breathing-may-be-the-secrets-to-surviving-2020/

[52] Oren Jay Sofer, Cultivating Authentic Communication, Session 1 January 31, 2021, pg 8.

[53] If you decide to make a bobblehead, here is a website that you can create your own: https://www.sharperimage.com/view/product/Custom+Bobble+Head/206631

[54] Rosenberg, Marshall. Non Violent Communication, page 196

[55] Rosenberg, Marshall. Non Violent Communication, page 197

www.ingramcontent.com/pod-product-compliance
Lightning Source LLC
Chambersburg PA
CBHW070706250726
48662CB00001B/284